ON HISTORY

Fig. 1. Tomb of Jules Michelet by Antonin Mercié, Père Lachaise cemetery, Paris.
Photo by Pierre-Yves Beaudouin,
http://commons.wikimedia.org/wiki/File:Père-Lachaise_-_Jules_Michelet_01.jpg.

Fig. 1. Tomb of Jules Michelet by Antonin Mercié, Père Lachaise cemetery, Paris.
Photo by Pierre-Yves Beaudouin,
http://commons.wikimedia.org/wiki/File:Père-Lachaise_-_Jules_Michelet_01.jpg.

ON HISTORY

www.ingramcontent.com/pod-product-compliance
Lightning Source LLC
Chambersburg PA
CBHW070849030726
47504CB00005B/1280

Open Book Classics

Jules Michelet

On History

Introduction to World History (1831)

Opening Address at the Faculty of
Letters, 9 January 1834

Preface to History of France (1869)

Translated by

Flora Kimmich, Lionel Gossman, and Edward K. Kaplan

Foreword

by Lionel Gossman

http://www.openbookpublishers.com

Digital material and resources associated with this volume are available on our website at: http://www.openbookpublishers.com/isbn/9781909254701

This is the first volume of the Open Book Classics series:

ISSN: 2054-216X (Print)
ISSN: 2054-2178 (Online)

ISBN Hardback: 978-1-909254-71-8
ISBN Paperback: 978-1-909254-70-1
ISBN Digital (PDF): 978-1-909254-72-5
ISBN Digital ebook (epub): 978-1-909254-73-2
ISBN Digital ebook (mobi): 978-1-909254-74-9

DOI: 10.11647/OBP.0036

Cover image: Jules Michelet, photograph by Félix Nadar (1850s), http://commons.wikimedia.org/wiki/File:Félix_Nadar_1820-1910_portraits_Jules_Michelet.jpg

All paper used by Open Book Publishers is SFI (Sustainable Forestry Initiative), and PEFC (Programme for the Endorsement of Forest Certification Schemes) Certified.

Printed in the United Kingdom and United States by Lightning Source for Open Book Publishers (Cambridge, UK).

Contents

Online supplements are available at
http://www.openbookpublishers.com/isbn/9781909254701:

1. John Stuart Mill, Review of M. Michelet, 'Histoire de France', *The Edinburgh Review*, January 1844, 159: 1-34.

2. Lionel Gossman, 'The Go-Between: Jules Michelet 1798-1874', *Modern Language Notes*, May 1974, 89/4: 503-541. © 1974, by kind permission of The Johns Hopkins University Press.

3. Lionel Gossman, 'Jules Michelet and Romantic Historiography,' *European Writers: The Romantic Century*, ed. Jacques Barzun (New York: Charles Scribner's Sons, 1985), pp 571-606. From Ed. George Stade. *Scribner Writers Online - European Writers Collection*. © 2010, by kind permission of Cengage Learning, Inc.

4. Lionel Gossman, 'Jules Michelet: National History, Biography, Autobiography.' Adapted from the article 'Jules Michelet: histoire nationale, biographie, autobiographie', *Littérature*, May, 1996, 102: 29-54.

5. Lionel Gossman, 'Michelet and Natural History: The Alibi of Nature', *Proceedings of the American Philosophical Society*, 3 September 2001, 145: 283-333. © 2001, by kind permission of the American Philosophical Society.

Contributors

Flora Kimmich translates from French and German. Her translation of Gustav Droysen's monumental nineteenth-century classic *History of Alexander the Great* [*Geschichte Alexanders des Grossen*]—the first into English—was published in 2012 by the American Philosophical Society.

Lionel Gossman, M. Taylor Pyne Professor emeritus of Romance Languages at Princeton University, is the author of books on Edward Gibbon, Augustin Thierry, Jacob Burckhardt, J.J. Bachofen, and the eighteenth-century French medievalist La Curne de Sainte-Palaye. He has also written on theoretical issues in historiography and on topics in European literature and cultural history.

Edward K. Kaplan is Kevy and Hortense Kaiserman Professor in the Humanities at Brandeis University. He is the author of two books and numerous articles on Michelet and the editor of *L'Insecte* and *L'Oiseau* in Paul Viallaneix's great 21-volume scholarly edition of Michelet's *Oeuvres complètes*. He has also published translations of Baudelaire as well as a biography and several influential studies of the modern Jewish theologian Abraham Heschel.

Acknowledgments

The editor is grateful to William St Clair of the School of Advanced Study, University of London, for wise counsel, in particular in relation to the Editor's Foreword; to Neil Rudenstine, former President of Harvard, for reminding him of Edmund Wilson's lifelong interest in Michelet; to his collaborators on the project, Flora Kimmich and Edward K. Kaplan, for their hard work and patience in translating complex and intricate texts; to Alessandra Tosi, Rupert Gatti, and Catherine Heygate of Open Book Publishers for their assistance in preparing the text for publication and to Corin Throsby for the cover design; and to the University Committee on Research in the Humanities and Social Sciences of Princeton University for contributing toward the cost of publication and thus helping to ensure unlimited access to scholarly work.

1. Foreword

Lionel Gossman

Michelet was the first modern historian to undertake to fill in the complete picture of the past, including science, art, literature, philosophy, architecture, costume and social habits, along with politics, war, religion, economics and law; and he makes you feel that he has actually been back to the Middle Ages or the Renaissance or the Reformation and returned with reactions as vivid as if he were dealing with contemporary events.

—Edmund Wilson, "Michelet," The New Republic, 31 August 1932

One of the great Romantic historians, Jules Michelet (1798-1874) served as model and inspiration for the founders of the influential *Annales* school of historians in France. As a result, he has had a more substantial impact on modern historiography than most of his contemporaries—than Carlyle (1795-1881), for example, or Macaulay (1800-1859) or Lamartine (1790-1869). The aim of the present volume, consisting of three relatively short, programmatic texts, is to convey to today's students of history in the English-speaking world, which the intense revival of interest in Michelet in France seems to have passed by, a sense of the nineteenth-century French historian's worldview and the values that underlie all his historiographical work—along with an idea of the way he conceived the shape of human history and envisaged the contribution the historian can make to human progress and wellbeing by promoting historical awareness and understanding. Taken together, the three texts can be read as a kind

DOI: 10.11647/OBP.0036.01

of manifesto of Romantic historiography. They do not purport to tell a particular story; they lay out a grand vision of history, what it means, why it matters, and why it is important for citizens to have a lively sense of it. Two—the *Introduction to World History* and the "Opening Address" at the Sorbonne of 1834—have been newly translated and are published here in English for the first time; the third, the great Preface to the 1869 edition of Michelet's complete, multi-volume *Histoire de France*, is a revised version, which the original translator has himself prepared, of the text he published, also for the first time in English, in his 1977 book, *Michelet's Poetic Vision: A Romantic Philosophy of Nature, Man & Woman* (Amherst: University of Massachusetts Press).[1]

Michelet was an extremely self-conscious historian: from the beginning to the end of his career he never ceased to reflect on history and historiography—what history writing had been in the past; what it could and should be in his own modern age; how it should respond to the political, social and cultural developments that had enabled the popular masses to come into their own, finally, as citizens of democratic nation-states; what structure and meaning might be discerned in history; and how, through a "comprehensive resurrection of the past" (*"résurrection intégrale du passé"*), the historian might contribute to the self-understanding, and hence to the emancipation and empowerment, of all humanity, of the various particular peoples composing it and of the individual human being (starting with himself)—inasmuch as the individual is part of a larger community, a product both of his nation's history and, beyond that, of the entire history of humanity. "I would like to explain to myself, as a modern man, my own birth," the 35-year-old professor told his young audience at the Sorbonne in 1834, for, as he wrote later to a friend, the journalist and literary scholar Eugène Noël, "I am France" (*"Je suis la France"*).[2] Michelet devoted an

---

1   Like the *Introduction à l'histoire universelle*, the Preface Michelet wrote in 1869 for a new 19-volume edition of his *Histoire de France* (originally published successively over the years from 1833 to 1867 in 17 volumes and covering the entire history of France down to the reign of Louis XVI), was not taken up in any of the English translations of this work. Most of these, in any case, did not venture beyond the volumes dealing with the period down to the late Middle Ages. It may be that the speculative and programmatic character of both texts was the cause of their having been neglected at a time when history was expected to be *"histoire événementielle"* ("a narrative of events"), to borrow the term invented by the *Annales* historians.

2   Letter of 2 January 1856, *Lettres inédites (1841-1871)*, ed. Paul Sirven (Paris: Presses Universitaires de France, 1924), p. 233.

impressive number of prefaces and essays, of which the present volume offers a modest sampling, to his reflection on those issues.

The first text in our volume, the *Introduction à l'histoire universelle*, outlines a very different view of World History from the traditional religious view represented, for instance, by Bossuet's celebrated *Discours sur l'histoire universelle* of 1681, even if the notion of Divine Providence is not completely obliterated and the perspective remains largely, though not exclusively Eurocentric. In Michelet's own words, "My first pages after the July Revolution, written on the burning cobblestones, were a vision of the world, of Universal History, as freedom's struggle, its ever-repeated victory over the world of determinism."[3]

Written in the immediate aftermath of the successful July Revolution of 1830, this essay presents in extraordinarily succinct and vivid form the basic dialectical structure and the richly metaphorical substance of Michelet's vision of history. In it the historian traces the world-historical process by which, from ancient times to the present, through immense, often violent and destructive struggles, periods of crisis, and clashes of cultures, the modern world was created, i.e. men and women gradually— often by the most devious routes—achieved ever greater freedom from the oppression of the strong and of material nature itself. The historian himself contributes to this process both by delving into the depths of the forgotten past and offering insight into hidden forces, fears, and impulses which determine the lives of the members of a community but of which they have hitherto been unaware, and by disclosing the pattern and direction of the history of humanity. Michelet represents this process as the progressive displacement of "fatality" by "freedom," of "matter" by "spirit," of myth by history, and, somewhat more problematically, of the female principle, that is to say, in his terms, of material necessity and the endlessly repeated

---

3   Preface to the 1869 edition of *History of France*. (See below) The idea of world history as a progressive movement toward ever greater human freedom and dignity had been proposed by Kant in his *Idee zu einer allgemeinen Geschichte in weltbürgerlicher Absicht* in 1784 and again by Schiller in his inaugural lecture, *Was heisst und zu welchem Ende studiert man Universalgeschichte?* at the University of Jena in 1789, and Michelet had read Schiller's short work in February 1828. ("Journal de mes lectures," in *Ecrits de jeunesse: Journal (1820-1823), Mémorial, Journal des idées*, ed. Paul Viallaneix [Paris: Gallimard, 1959], p. 329) But Kant and Schiller were calling for a history that they themselves believed would be difficult, if not impossible to write and that they did not even sketch out in its broad lines. In addition, the point of view of both Kant and Schiller was that of the cosmopolitan Enlightenment. Neither had Michelet's keen interest in the particular character and contribution of different peoples or his insight into the complexities of an historical development often promoted by seemingly "reactionary" and "unenlightened" behaviours and actions.

cycle of birth and death, by the ever-expanding power of reason, law and scientific understanding.[4] History, it could be said, liberates man from the past, inasmuch as the past is like the womb in which the preconscious infant is nurtured, the breast at which he is fed and from which he must detach himself in order to become a free, active and independent individual in charge of his own destiny. What results from the triumph of the male principle, Michelet emphasizes, is not a new tyranny of men over women, or of spirit over nature, but a "penetration" of the female by the male principle, the liberation of woman herself from the tyranny of her own bodily nature, and the humanisation of nature, its transformation from a blind and indifferent determinism into an ally and partner of "spirit." Within this world history is embedded the history of France, which is portrayed as at once emblematic and exemplary. Whence the claim at the end of the essay that France is the nation that, after the glorious July Revolution of 1830, is destined to lead all humanity on the next stage of its unending journey to ever greater freedom and dominion over nature and fate. Michelet adhered to this program throughout all his writing, including even the remarkable and best-selling natural histories, to which he turned in his later years, after being removed in 1852, on political grounds, from his positions at the Collège de France and the National Archives.[5]

Though twice as long as the *Introduction* itself (an effect of Michelet's fascination with Germany and German scholarship?), the extensive "Notes and Clarifications" appended to it, some of which amount to virtual essays in their own right, have been included in order to give a sense of the range of Michelet's interests and reading.[6] As befitted his conception of history, he was not content simply to adapt and revise traditional historical narratives. He knew that in order to write the totally new kind of history he envisaged, a history embracing all aspects of people's lives, he would have to exploit

---

4   Cf. John Stuart Mill's comment on the "brilliant sketch" of the various provinces of France — the celebrated "Tableau de la France" — at the beginning of volume II of the *Histoire de France*: "A strenuous asserter of the power of mind over matter, of will over spontaneous propensities, culture over nature, [Michelet] holds that local characteristics lose their importance as history advances. In a rude age the 'fatalities' of race and geographical position are absolute. In the progress of society, human forethought and purpose, acting by means of uniform institutions and modes of culture, tend more and more to efface the pristine differences." (Mill, "Michelet's History of France," in J.S. Mill, *Collected Works*, ed. Jean O'Grady and John M. Robson [Toronto: University of Toronto Press; London: Routledge, 1963-1991], vol. 20, p. 238) See the full text of Mill's review in the Online Supplement.

5   See the essays "The Go-Between: Jules Michelet 1798-1874" and "Michelet and Natural History: The Alibi of Nature" in the Online Supplement.

6   On Michelet's wide reading, see also the "Journal de mes lectures," pp. 301-331.

a wide range of sources: archival documents, to which, as Director of the Historical Section of the National Archives, he had ready access until 1852; scholarly works in various languages from the Renaissance to his own time, including quite recent books on the Orient and editions of ancient Oriental literature; the writings of the Ancients (Greek and Latin); the great texts of medieval and modern European literature from Dante to Goethe and Byron; popular literature and folk tales; works of art and architecture; studies of religion, law, and medicine; and rules and precepts for the conduct of daily life.

Michelet's inaugural lecture or "Opening Address" as Professor of History, on 9 January 1834, to a packed auditorium at the Sorbonne, on his temporarily replacing Guizot, who had been appointed Minister of Education in the new government of Louis-Philippe, is the second text in our volume. In it Michelet again argues for the importance of the study of history, impressing on his young audience that the present is the product of the past, which is always alive within it, that every human being carries an immense past within himself (Michelet was addressing an almost exclusively male audience) of which he often has little or no consciousness, and that it is the task of the historian to bring that unconscious foundation of the living individual to the light of consciousness. This is at one and the same time an act of piety toward those past generations on whose sufferings and sacrifices the present has been built (history as *"résurrection"*) and a step forward in the emancipation of the present generation. Taking up, in even more concentrated form, the broad outlines of the *Introduction to World History*, but focusing on one particular period of crisis and transition in the fourteenth and fifteenth centuries (developed more fully shortly afterwards in volume III [1837] of the *Histoire de France*), the lecturer called on his audience to learn from history that humanity's grand progressive movement has often been realised through crises so severe and disorienting that many believed the end of the world was imminent. In fact, what the people of the fourteenth and fifteenth centuries were living through was the end of the Middle Ages, the prelude to a new and brighter time for all humanity. In a similar way, the students were doubtless expected to understand, the turmoil of the end of the Ancien Régime, the Revolution, and the Restoration, which they were living through, was the prelude to a new and better future. Informed by history, the young should therefore have confidence in the essentially progressive character of the historical process, through times of seemingly catastrophic upheavals and disasters, and should work to promote that process, never yielding to passivity or despair. The lecture was received by its young audience with enthusiastic and prolonged applause.

The third work presented here, the beautiful Preface Michelet wrote for a new edition of his complete *Histoire de France* in 1869, presents a retrospective account of how the historian's understanding of French history evolved in the course of writing the successive volumes of the *Histoire de France*, together with his view of the goals of historical writing, the methods by which those goals can be attained, and his own evolving relation, as its historian, to the object of his research and writing. The translator has himself provided an Introduction to this remarkable text. Its combination of boldly original and imaginative writing style and probing reflection and analysis is characteristic of Michelet's mature work.

Though separated by almost four decades, the three texts, taken together, constitute a powerful statement of a great historian's vision of history and of the importance, for the present, of investigating, exhuming, and understanding the past in all its richness and complexity.

***

After falling into disfavour and being regarded with disdain as "literary" by the positivist historians who followed him, Michelet was rediscovered and rehabilitated in the early twentieth century by the members of the *Annales* school, notably Lucien Febvre and Marc Bloch, the school's founders, and Fernand Braudel, one of its most prominent and widely admired later leaders. Febvre refers frequently to Michelet in his own work and from December 1942 to April 1943, in the darkest days of the German occupation of France, he devoted an entire lecture course at the Collège de France to his nineteenth-century predecessor's account of the Renaissance. This was followed by another course, in 1943-1944, dedicated to Michelet as a renovator of history. Febvre also brought out a little volume on Michelet soon after the end of the War: *Michelet 1798-1874* (Geneva: Éditions des Trois Collines, 1946), in which he defended Michelet as "the founding model" of modern French historiography and took issue with those who still held that "as a historian, he wasn't so great."[7] In 1992, over three decades after Febvre's death, his 1942-1943

---

7   *Michelet 1798-1874*, Introduction and choice of texts by Lucien Febvre, p. 11. (All translations in the Editor's Foreword are by the editor unless otherwise indicated.) On Michelet as the *modèle fondateur* of the *Annales* school, see Florence Hulak, *Sociéte et mentalité*.

lectures, edited by Fernand Braudel, were published by Flammarion as *Michelet et la Renaissance*. In Febvre's words, "The historical method of the Michelet of 1840 can be defined in two words: it is totalizing and it is synthesizing" ("*elle est totalitaire et elle est synthétique*"). "It is totalizing because it does not assign to the historian the task of reviving any one of the multiple activities in which human beings are engaged—political activity, for example, or the law, or religion. All things human matter to the historian, everything men create or do is the object of history [...]: political constitutions, churches, religions or philosophies, artistic or literary productions, economic activities, scientific discoveries. It is synthesizing because it is not enough for the historian to study political history, or the history of law, or the history of art separately. [...] Everything to do with human beings must be studied together. For there is no single work of men that does not have an impact on all the others both severally and taken together."[8] This view of Michelet's significance was echoed by the medievalist Jacques Le Goff, a younger member of the *Annales* school. Michelet, Le Goff claimed, is "the father of the new history, of a total history that aims to grasp the past in all its density" ("*le père de l'histoire nouvelle, de l'histoire totale qui veut saisir le passé dans toute son épaisseur*").[9] Marc Bloch was somewhat more circumspect than his colleague Febvre: "Michelet is a seductive, but sometimes dangerous model," he warned ("*Michelet est un maître séduisant, mais parfois dangereux*"). Nevertheless, Michelet and Fustel de Coulanges were, for him too, "our great forebears,"

La science historique de Marc Bloch (Paris: Hermann, 2012), pp. 13, 99. Even in the positivist period of French historiography, some eminent historians, notably Gabriel Monod, who had known Michelet personally, continued to admire and be inspired by him; see Monod's essays on Michelet in his *Les Maîtres de l'histoire: Renan, Taine, Michelet* (Paris: Calmann Lévy, 1894), pp. 185-269 and *Portraits et souvenirs* (Paris: Calmann Lévy, 1897), pp. 15-59; his *Jules Michelet* (Paris: Sandoz et Fischbacher, 1875) and his two major studies, *Jules Michelet, Études sur sa vie et ses oeuvres avec des fragments inédits* (Paris: Hachette, 1905) and *La Vie et la pensée de Jules Michelet* (Paris: Champion, 1923), 2 vols. (the text of a course taught at the Collège de France in 1905-1910).

8   Lucien Febvre, *Michelet et la Renaissance* (Paris: Flammarion, 1992), p. 108. See, below, the opening pages of Michelet's Preface to the 1869 edition of the *Histoire de France*.

9   Jacques Le Goff, "Michelet et le Moyen Âge aujourd'hui," in Michelet, *Oeuvres complètes*, ed. Paul Viallaneix (Paris: Flammarion, 1971-1987), 21 vols., vol. 4, pp. 45-63. According to Le Goff, Michelet's vision of a total history of the Middle Ages—a history that would emerge from "all possible documents, laws and art, charters and poems, the soil and libraries, a history that would exploit the entire arsenal of the human sciences (not available to Michelet but called for by his method) and that would resuscitate not ghosts but real people of flesh and also of intellect and feeling"—remains a challenge to modern-day medievalists, many of whom are still caught up in narrow issues of erudition and do not venture beyond their special fields of research. (p. 60)

who "taught us to recognize that the object of history is, by its nature, man."[10]

For his part, Fernand Braudel saluted Michelet in his inaugural lecture at the Collège de France on 1 December 1950, as "the greatest of all" the nineteenth-century historians—greater even than Ranke or Burckhardt—in recognition of "so many flashes of insight and inspired premonitions" (*"tant d'éclairs et de prémonitions géniales"*).[11] Four years later the prestigious Paris publishing house of Les Éditions du Seuil brought out *Michelet par lui-même*, a selection of texts with commentaries by the late Roland Barthes. This penetrating and innovative study by the leading avant-garde French literary critic of the second half of the twentieth century has now acquired classic status and continues to be reprinted by the publisher. In it Barthes takes up Febvre's theme of Michelet as the pioneer of total history. The historian's much derided "subjectivity," he argues, was in fact "the earliest form of an insistence on totality" and the nineteenth-century Romantic turns out to have been "at once a sociologist, an ethnologist, a psychoanalyst, and a social historian."[12] Even if he often interpreted them symbolically, as one means of establishing interconnections among them, the objects of Michelet's interest—climatic and geographical conditions, popular mentalities, eating habits, clothing, health and disease, arts and

---

10   Marc Bloch, review of Febvre's *Histoire de la Franche-Comté*, *Revue de Synthèse*, 28 (1914): 354; Bloch, *The Historian's Craft*, translated by Peter Putnam (New York: Vintage Books, 1953), p. 25.

11   Fernand Braudel, *Écrits sur l'histoire* (Paris: Flammarion, 1969), pp. 15-38, on p. 19.

12   "His subjectivity was only the earliest form of that insistence on totality, those authentic comparisons and associations, that attention to the most insignificant concrete detail, that today characterize the very method of the human sciences. It is because Michelet was a discredited historian—from a positivist point of view—that he could be at once a sociologist, an ethnologist, a psychoanalyst, a social historian." (Roland Barthes, Preface to his edition of Michelet's *La Sorcière* [Paris: Club Français du Livre, 1959], reprinted in *Essais Critiques* [Paris: Éditions du Seuil, 1964], p. 124) The idea of a history embracing more than politics and the actions of the great had, of course, been put forward by many Enlightenment writers. Friedrich Schiller, for instance, conceived of something close to the "total history" that, according to Febvre or Barthes, had been Michelet's goal. "In truth," Schiller wrote, "the history of religion and the churches, the history of philosophy, the history of art, of customs and manners, and the history of trade and commerce ought to be consolidated with political history. Only such a history would be a true world history." (Cited in Friedrich Burschell, *Schiller* [Reinbek bei Hamburg: Rowohlt, 1968], p. 295) But this remained an ideal. In practice, the story of the underground dwellings that ants build for themselves in silence while eagles and vultures tear each other apart in the air above them, as Voltaire put it, was usually conceived as distinct from other activities and was confined in the work of Voltaire and Hume to separate chapters, isolated from the main narrative. Nor was the Enlightenment historian sensitive to the interest of "the most insignificant concrete detail."

technologies, the historian's relation to the objects of his study—have indeed come to occupy a central place in modern historical research.

Reflecting the revived interest in Michelet among French historians, new editions of his major works, the *Histoire de France* and the *Histoire de la Révolution Française*, have been published in the last half-century—the former in several multi-volume editions, with various publishers, between 1964 and 2009, as well as in a cheap popular paperback abridgement in 1963, the latter in two volumes of over 1500 pages each in Gallimard's elegant *Bibliothèque de la Pléaide* collection in 1952, in a 6-volume edition in 1967, a 7-volume edition in 1974, a 9-volume edition in 1979, as well as in several abridgements, including one in the popular *Livre de Poche* series on the eve of the bicentenary of the Revolution. In addition, many individual works, such as the *Mémoires de Luther*, the *Histoire romaine*, *Le Peuple*, *La Sorcière*, *La Femme*, *Légendes démocratiques du Nord*, *Le Procès des Templiers* and the inevitable *Jeanne d'Arc*, not to mention the natural history writings of the historian's later years, have been republished in the last half-century, while hitherto private writings and unpublished lectures have also been edited and made available to contemporary scholars: the early diaries (*Écrits de jeunesse*, 1959), the astounding *Journal* to which Michelet confided both his most intimate thoughts and fantasies and his reflections on history and plans for historical writing (4 vols., 1959-1976); the *Correspondance générale* (12 vols., 1994-2001); the lectures delivered at the École Normale (1987); and the courses taught at the Collège de France from 1838 to 1851 (2 vols., 1995). Between 1971 and 1987 the publishing house of Flammarion put out Paul Viallaneix's magisterial 21-volume edition of Michelet's *Oeuvres complètes*.

***

In Michelet's own lifetime, virtually every one of his works appeared in English translation, both in England and in the United States, soon after its publication in French, and all the translations went through several editions. The natural history books that the historian began to produce in collaboration with his second wife, Athénaïs Mialaret, after he had been dismissed, on refusing to take the oath of allegiance to Napoleon III, from his positions at the Collège de France and the National Archives, proved especially popular in the English-speaking world. The regular historical writings were by no means neglected, however. Though John Stuart Mill, who admired and corresponded (indirectly) with Michelet, expressed regret in 1840 that the French historian, "a writer of great and original

views," was "very little known among us,"[13] an English translation of the
early *Précis de l'histoire moderne* (1827-1828) was in fact adopted for use in
schools and colleges,[14] and two different translations of the first volumes
of the *Histoire de France* were published simultaneously in the late 1840s by
different London publishing houses.[15] The English translation of the first
four books of the *Histoire de la Révolution Française*, went through at least
five editions between its first publication in 1848 and the end of the century.
Mill certainly did his bit to make Michelet better known. He himself wrote a
long, extremely favourable review of the *Histoire de France* for the influential
Edinburgh Review in 1844; he arranged for his "young friend," George Henry
Lewes, the longtime partner of the novelist George Eliot, and a great admirer
of Michelet, whose work he helped to have translated into English, to meet
personally with the historian in Paris; and he encouraged Lewes to write
an article on the contemporary French historians — including Michelet, "the
historian *par excellence*" in Lewes' words — in the *British and Foreign Review*,
also in 1844.[16] "Michelet's books," Mill wrote, "are not for those who dislike
to think or explore for themselves," they are "not books to save a reader the
trouble of thinking, but to make him boil over with thought. Their effect on
the mind is not acquiescence, but stir and ferment."[17]

   While the rediscovery of Michelet by modern French historians has
led to the publication of many new editions of his writings over the last
half-century in France, there has been, in contrast, a marked decline in

13 Letter to Macvey Napier, 27 April 1840, "The Earlier Letters of John Stuart Mill 1812-1848,"
in Mill, *Collected Works*, vol. 13, p. 431.
14 A. Potter, D.D., of Union College, the author of the Introduction to an 1843 edition of
this work put out by Harper and Brothers in New York and entitled *Modern History*, salutes
Michelet, "one of the most learned, laborious, and elegant" of the "remarkable school" of
recent French historians, for combining "great philosophical sagacity" with "what is so apt
to be wanting in the German historians — a brilliant imagination, a clear and picturesque
style, and great felicity of illustration." He then defines the intended readership of the
pocket-sized work: "While this work will be useful to general readers, its more immediate
object is to furnish a good text-book in modern history for schools and colleges." *Modern
History*, it turns out, went through eight editions, with various publishers in London and
New York, between 1843 and 1900. As late as 1911, the otherwise severely critical author
of the article on Michelet in the 11ᵗʰ edition of the *Encyclopaedia Britannica* (vol. 18, p. 369)
considered this early work "a sound and careful book, far better than anything that had
appeared before it, and written in a sober yet interesting style."
15 *History of France*, translated by Walter K. Kelly (London: Chapman and Hall, 1844-1846);
History of France, translated by G.H. Smith (London: Whittaker, 1844-1847; New York: Appleton,
1845-1848).
16 Mill in *Edinburgh Review*, 79 (January 1844): 1-39; Lewes in *British and Foreign Review*, 16
(January 1844): 72-118, quoted phrase on p. 105.
17 *Edinburgh Review* article, reproduced in Mill, *Collected Works*, vol. 20, pp. 217-255, on p. 231.

English-language publications of his work since 1900. To the degree that he figures at all in the historiographical landscape of English-speaking scholars, he is usually thought of, above all, as an excessively literary and "imaginative" historian, strongly nationalist and anglophobic, who claimed a privileged place for his country in world history.[18] Even in the nineteenth century the later volumes of the *Histoire de France* aroused far less interest than the earlier ones on the Middle Ages, and where they were discussed they were subject to harsh criticism, provoked partly no doubt by the increasingly strident anti-English strain in those later volumes and partly by a tone of unconcealed political and moral engagement in them that ran counter to the "neutrality" required by the positivist ideal of a politically more conservative generation. By 1911, the author of the article on Michelet in the 11th edition of the *Encyclopaedia Britannica* noted that Michelet of late had "not received much attention from critics and monographers." His own judgment was severe. "The *Introduction à l'histoire universelle*," he wrote "showed a different style" from that of the earlier *Précis de l'histoire moderne,* "exhibiting no doubt the idiosyncracy and literary power of the writer to greater advantage but also displaying the peculiar visionary qualities which made him the most stimulating, but the most untrustworthy (not in facts,

---

18 Michelet himself vigorously rejected the view that he was essentially a "literary" and "imaginative" writer. On learning that Mill was planning to write a review of his *Histoire de France*, he penned this note: "Should Mr. Mill do me the honour of reviewing my book in an English journal, I would be most obliged to him if he would emphasize how powerfully this historian, too thoughtlessly accounted a 'man of the imagination,' has been motivated by a passion for the *truth*." The English reading public should be made aware that his account of the trial of Joan of Arc, for instance, is based not on chronicle sources but on documents; and he counts on "the impartiality of an Englishman" to defend his book, despite the fact that it "presents so unfavourable a view of the English." (Letter to Gustave d'Eichthal, 24 September 1841, *Correspondance générale*, ed. Louis Le Guillou, vol. 3 [Paris: Champion, 1995], pp. 480-481) See also Michelet's letter to Taine, complaining that the praise heaped on him as a writer is part of a campaign to diminish him as a historian (cited in Roland Barthes, *Michelet par lui-même* [Paris: Éditions du Seuil, 1969], p. 89) and a long letter of late July 1911 in which Lucien Febvre defends Michelet for having distinguished carefully between "l'art" and "l'histoire" against Henri Berr, founder of the *Revue de Synthèse*, who lumped Michelet and Thierry together as "poets" who both "created and deformed history." (Lucien Febvre, *De la 'Revue de synthèse' aux 'Annales': Lettres à Henri Berr, 1911-1954* [Paris: Fayard, 1997], p. 10) Even as a writer, however, Michelet's vivid, emphatic style came in for severe criticism from modern anti-Romantics; e.g. Paul Valéry: "By chance, have been reading some Michelet. [...] It gave me a fit of *literary* indignation. That stuff is made to be preached in some popular university; there's not a word in it worth *reflection*. [...] All that claptrap has never been *put through* the intellect (it would have come to pieces and dissolved), but merely blurted out to the superficial public." (Letter to André Gide, 5 July 1908, in Paul Valéry, *History and Politics*, translated by Denise Folliot and Jackson Mathews [New York: Pantheon Books, 1962], p. 512)

which he never consciously falsifies, but in suggestion) of all historians." As for his *Histoire de la Révolution*, "in actual picturesqueness as well as in general veracity of picture, the book cannot approach Carlyle's, while as a mere chronicle of events it is inferior to half a dozen prosaic histories older and younger than itself."[19]

Thanks to Edmund Wilson's widely read and now classic *To the Finland Station* (1940), Michelet did make a brilliant but brief reappearance on the Anglo-American literary and intellectual scene in the mid-twentieth century. Unusually—for, as Wilson put it himself in the early 1930s, "Michelet's 'History of France' was popular with our grandfathers, but people seem rarely to read it today"—Wilson and his mother had read Michelet together when he was a young man, and he relates that he carried the memory of the chapters on Philip the Bold with him while serving in Eastern France in World War I.[20] Later he came to admire Michelet as a historian to whom the writing of history had been a way of acting on history, and it was as a critic of the decline of the revolutionary tradition and an advocate of "the idea that society can be remade by men in accord with human aspiration"[21] that he published a short laudatory article on Michelet in the old, progressive *New Republic* in 1932 and turned again to the nineteenth-century French historian for the first five chapters of *To the Finland Station*, his comprehensive account of the revolutionary idea from the early nineteenth century to the October Revolution. If "Michelet is no longer read," he asserted, referring to an article written in France in 1898, on the eve of the Michelet centenary, it is

> because people no longer understand him. [...] He commits for the skeptical young men of the end of the century the supreme sin of being an apostle, a man of passionate feeling and conviction. Michelet created the religion of the Revolution and the Revolution is not popular today, when the Academicians put it in its place, when persons who would have been nothing without it veil their faces at the thought of the Jacobin terror, when even those who have nothing against it manage to patronize it.[22]

---

19   *Encyclopaedia Britannica*, 11th edn. (Cambridge, 1911), vol. 18, pp. 369-70.
20   Edmund Wilson, "Michelet," *The New Republic*, 31 August 1932; Lewis M. Dabney, *Edmund Wilson: A Life in Literature* (New York: Farrar, Strauss and Giroux, 2005), p. 14; Edmund Wilson, *Literary Essays and Reviews of the 1920s and 30s*, ed. Lewis M. Dabney (New York: Library of America, 2007), p. 576.
21   Dabney, *Edmund Wilson*, p. 254.
22   Edmund Wilson, To *the Finland Station: A Study in the Writing and Acting of History* (New York: Harcourt Brace, 1940), p. 37

In addition to Michelet's fervent engagement with history, Wilson also emphasized his originality as a historian,

> fusing disparate materials, [...] indicating the interrelations between the different forms of human activity [...] as if he were braiding a rope. [...] Yet the plaiting of a rope is too coarse an image. No image except that of life itself can convey the penetrating intelligence with which, in the volumes on Louis XIV, for example, Michelet interrelates the intrigues of the court, the subjects of Molière's comedies and the economic condition of France.[23]

Wilson's enthusiastic endorsement of Michelet was unusual, however, if not unique, and as he was himself a man of letters—essayist, critic, and novelist (and socialist at the time to boot)—rather than a professional historian, it appears to have done little to enhance awareness of or interest in Michelet among practising historians in the English-speaking world.

In 1967, as part of a series devoted to pre-twentieth century classics of historiography, a much abridged version of the 1848 translation of the *History of the French Revolution* was put out by the University of Chicago Press.[24] It is not clear, however, what impact, if any, this publication has had, and an attempt in 1972 by a small press in Pennsylvania to publish the complete *History of the French Revolution* in a new translation seems to have faltered after the appearance of three non-consecutive volumes (4, 6, and 7).[25] The University of Illinois Press brought out a translation of *Le Peuple* in 1973. Increasing attention to women's history also sparked a revival of interest in *La Sorcière (The Witch)*, and 1987 saw the publication in New York of Roland Barthes' book on Michelet in a translation by the gifted poet and essayist Richard Howard. It seems highly likely, however, that the appearance of Howard's translation had more to do with the reputation of Barthes among literary scholars than with interest in Michelet among historians. There have been a few fine studies of Michelet and his work in English, but these have also mostly been by literary scholars rather than historians. (See the bibliography at the end of this volume.)

---

23 Wilson, *To the Finland Station*, pp. 18, 20.

24 Based on the 1848 translation by Charles Cocks, the Professor of English at the Collège Royal in Paris, and updated by the editor, Stanford Professor Gordon Wright, this edition contained only the Introduction and the first three of the twenty-one books of the original, ending on the account of the Fête de la Fédération (14 July 1790). Cocks's 1848 translation, which included as much of the text as had been published in France at the time (publication of the entire work in French was not completed until 1853), had also included Book IV. The last edition to be reviewed and revised by Michelet himself appeared in 1869.

25 Wynnewood, PA: Kolokol Press, 1972-1973. The three volumes contained Books 7-8, 11-13 and 14-17 of Michelet's text.

Michelet, it would seem, cuts a very small figure on the historiographical horizon of the English-speaking world. It is hoped that the present volume will revive interest in a nineteenth-century historian who was hailed by the leaders of the modern *Annales* school as a founding father.

2. Chronology of Jules Michelet[1]

1798   Born in Paris. 16 rue de Tracy, near the Porte Saint-Denis. Father a master printer; mother, Angélique-Constance Millet, from a well-to-do peasant family in Renwez (Ardennes).

1808   Father imprisoned for debt.

1808-1809   Works in his father's printing shop.

1812-1816   Student at Collège (now Lycée) Charlemagne.

1815   Death of his mother.

1816   Baptised. Wins three prizes in the *Concours général*, a national competition for students in the penultimate and final classes of colleges and lycées.

1817   *Baccalauréat*. Assistant teacher at Institution Briand.

1818   *Licence*.

1819   *Doctorat ès Lettres*.

1821   Passes *Agrégation*, a competitive examination that entitles those who have passed it to teach in public institutions of higher education.

1822-1827   Professor of History at Collège Sainte Barbe in Paris.

1824   Marriage to Pauline Rousseau (20 May); birth of daughter Adèle (28 August).

1824   Encouraged by his teacher, Victor Cousin, undertakes to translate Vico's *La Scienza nuova*.

1825   Makes the acquaintance of Edgar Quinet through Victor Cousin.

1825   **Tableau chronologique de l'Histoire de France**.

1826   Applies for chair at École Normale.

1826   **Tableau synchronique de l'Histoire Moderne**.

---

1   Major works are marked in bold.

DOI: 10.11647/OBP.0036.02

1827	Apppointed Professor of Philosophy and History at École Normale.
1827	*Principes de la Philosophie de l'Histoire* (his translation of Vico).
1827	*Précis de l'Histoire Moderne*, vol. 1.
1828	Travels to Germany. Appointed tutor to the Princesse de Berry, grand-daughter of Charles X, the last Bourbon king.
1828	*Précis de l'Histoire Moderne*, vol. 2.
1829	Birth of Michelet's son Charles.
1830	Travels in Italy. July Revolution. Charles X flees and Louis-Philippe assumes the throne. Michelet appointed Head of the History Section of the Archives Nationales. Also appointed tutor to Princesse Clémentine, youngest daughter of Louis-Philippe.
1831	*Introduction à l'Histoire Universelle.*
1831	*Histoire Romaine*, vols. I, II.
1833	*Précis de l'Histoire de France.*
1833	*Histoire de France*, vols. I, II (until 1270).
1834-1835	Serves as substitute professor at the Sorbonne for François Guizot, who had been appointed Minister of Education.
1834	Travels to England.
1835	*Mémoires de Luther.*
1837	Travels to Belgium and Holland.
1837	*Histoire de France*, vol. III (1270-1380).
1837	*Origines du droit français.*
1838	Appointed Professor at Collège de France. Gives up his position at the École Normale. Elected to Académie des Sciences morales et politiques. Visits Venice.
1839	Visits Lyon. Death of Pauline.
1840	Establishes a relationship with Mme Dumesnil; becomes colleague of Polish Romantic and national poet Adam Mickiewicz on latter's appointment to Chair of Slavic Literature at Collège de France. Travels to Belgium.
1840	*Histoire de France*, vol. IV (1380-1422).
1841	Edgar Quinet appointed Professor of Languages and Literatures of Southern Europe at Collège de France. Michelet, Quinet and Mickiewicz close colleagues and friends.
1841	*Procès des Templiers*, vol. I. Collection de documents inédits sur l'histoire de France.
1841	*Histoire de France*, vol. V (Joan of Arc).

1842	Death of Mme Dumesnil. Travels to Germany.
1843	Michelet resigns from his position as tutor to the royal princesses. His daughter Adèle marries his favorite student, Alfred Dumesnil, the son of his former lover. Travels to Switzerland.
1843	*Les Jésuites*, written in collaboration with Edgar Quinet.
1844	*Histoire de France*, vol. VI (Louis XI).
1845	Clerical campaign directed against Michelet's teaching at Collège de France.
1845	*Du prêtre, de la femme et de la famille.*
1846	Death of Michelet's father, who had lived with him since the death of his mother in 1815.
1846	*Le Peuple.*
1847	*Histoire de la Révolution française*, vols. I, II.
1848	Michelet's course at Collège de France suspended on charge of fomenting revolutionary unrest. Revolution of February 1848. Michelet's course reinstated in triumph in March. Athénaïs Mialaret arrives in Paris with intention of being Michelet's disciple. Louis-Napoleon Bonaparte elected President of France's Second Republic in December.
1849	Marriage of Michelet and Athénaïs Mialaret.
1849	*Histoire de la Révolution française*, vol. III.
1850	Birth and death of the Michelets' infant son, given the name Yves-Jean-Lazare.
1850	*Histoire de la Révolution française*, vol. IV.
1851	Anti-government demonstrations among students at Michelet's lectures. Michelet's course suspended. Coup d'état of Napoleon, who becomes Napoleon III.
1851	*Procès des Templiers*, vol. II.
1851	*Histoire de la Révolution française*, vol. V.
1852	Michelet refuses to swear oath of allegiance to Napoleon III and is dismissed from his positions at the Collège de France and at the Archives Nationales.
1853-1854	The Michelets go into exile in Italy (Nervi, Genoa, Turin).
1853	*Histoire de la Révolution française*, vol. VI.
1854	The Michelets return to Paris but are henceforth frequently absent from the capital—both in the French provinces and abroad, chiefly in Switzerland.

1854	*Légendes démocratiques du Nord.*
1854	*Les Femmes de la Révolution.*
1855	Death of Michelet's daughter Adèle.
1855	*Histoire de France*, vols. VII (Renaissance) and VIII (Reformation).
1856	*Histoire de France*, vols. IX (Wars of Religion) and X (The League).
1856	*L'Oiseau.* (First of many highly successful books on topics of natural history. Having no official post, Michelet now has to earn a living from his writing).
1857	*Histoire de France*, vol. XI (Henri IV).
1857	*L'Insecte.*
1858	*Histoire de France*, vol. XII (Louis XIII).
1858	*L'Amour.*
1859	*La Femme.*
1860	*Histoire de France*, vol. XIII (Louis XIV).
1861	*La Mer.*
1862	Death of Michelet's son Charles, who never amounted to much and to whom he was never close.
1862	*Histoire de France*, vol. XIV (Louis XIV).
1862	*La Sorcière.*
1863	*Histoire de France*, vol. XV (Regency of Duc d'Orléans).
1864	*La Bible de l'Humanité.*
1866	*Histoire de France*, vol. XVI (Louis XV).
1867	*Histoire de France*, vol. XVII (Louis XVI).
1868	*La Montagne.*
1869	New Prefaces for *Histoire de France* and *Histoire de la Révolution.*
1869	*Nos Fils.*
1870	Franco-Prussian War. The Michelets move to Italy. Michelet suffers attacks of apoplexy in Pisa and Florence. The couple visit Switzerland, then move to Hyères in the South of France, near the Mediterranean.
1871	*La France devant l'Europe.*
1872	*Histoire du XIXᵉ siècle*, vol. I.
1873	*Histoire du XIXᵉ siècle*, vol. II.
1874	Death of Michelet at Hyères.
1874	*Histoire du XIXᵉ siècle*, vol. III.
1876	Michelet's remains transferred to Paris and buried at Père-Lachaise.

3. Introduction to World History

Jules Michelet

Translated by Flora Kimmich[1]

1   This translation is based upon the following edition: J. Michelet, *Introduction à l'histoire universelle, suivi du Discours d'ouverture prononcé à la Faculté des Lettres le 9 janvier 1834* (Paris: Librairie Classique de L. Hachette, 1834). It has been checked against the first edition of April 1831 (with the same publisher), available at http://gallica.bnf.fr/ark:/12148/btv1b8626729v

DOI: 10.11647/OBP.0036.03

Fig. 2. Jules Michelet, circa 1842, after a drawing by Thomas Couture, reproduced
in Jules Michelet, *Lettres inédites* (1841-1871),
ed. Paul Sirven (Paris: Presses Universitaires de France, 1924), frontispiece.

With the world, a war began that will end with the world, and not before: the war of man against nature, of spirit against matter, of liberty against fatality. History is nothing but the story of this endless struggle.

In recent years fatality has seemed to be taking possession of knowledge no less than of the world. It has been quietly infiltrating philosophy and history. Liberty has demanded its place in society; it is time for it to claim its place in knowledge too. If this introduction achieves its aim, history will be revealed as an enduring protest, as the progressive triumph of liberty.

Liberty has its limits, no doubt; I do not intend to dispute them. I am only too aware of them in the way physical nature works to consume man. I feel them even more keenly in the turmoil that this enemy world raises in me. Amid the threats and allurements with which the world besets us, who has not repudiated and denied liberty a hundred times. *Eppur si muove*, as Galileo said. No matter what I do, I discover there is something in me that will not yield, that will not accept the yoke of either man or nature, that submits to reason alone, to law alone, and will not make peace with fatality. May that struggle go on forever! For it is the dignity of man and the very harmony of the world.

And it will go on, without any doubt, for as long as human will braces itself against the influence of race and climate, for as long as a Byron can leave industrial England to live in Italy and die in Greece, for as long as the soldiers of France shall march out and pitch camp, be it on the Vistula or the Tiber, in the name of universal liberty.[1]

What should hearten us in this endless struggle is that, on the whole, the odds are in our favor. Of the two adversaries, one never changes, the other changes and becomes stronger. Nature remains the same, while man daily gains some advantage of her. The Alps have grown no higher, while we have cut our way through the Simplon. The winds and the tides are as

---

1   This was written in January 1830. I have not had the heart to remove it. [Footnotes are Michelet's unless otherwise indicated]

treacherous as ever, but the steamship plows the main with no thought of capricious winds and seas.

Trace the movements of humankind from east to west along the path of the sun and the magnetic currents of the globe, observe humankind on this long journey from Asia to Europe, from India to France, and you will see at every station on the way how the fatal power of nature diminishes and the influence of race and climate becomes less tyrannical. At the point of departure, in India, in the cradle of all races and religions—*the womb of the world*—man is bent, prostrated beneath all-powerful nature. He is a helpless baby at his mother's breast, a frail, dependent creature, coddled and beaten by turns, more intoxicated than nourished by a milk too strong for him. Nature holds him languishing, bathed in hot, humid air heavy with the perfumes of powerful aromatics. His strength, his life, his mind succumb. Man is no stronger for being multiplied in excess and squandered, as it were, with heedless disregard: in such climates life and death wield equal power. In Benares the earth yields three harvests each year. Torrential rains turn a moor into a meadow. The reed of that land is the sixty-foot bamboo. The tree is the Indian fig, which produces a forest from a single root. Under these monstrous plants, monsters roam. The tiger lurks on the riverbank, stalking the hippopotamus, which it seizes in a single bound of ten times six feet. A herd of wild elephants storms through the forest, toppling trees left and right. And all the while, terrifying storms remove mountains and cholera morbus mows down millions.

Meeting disproportionate force everywhere, crushed by nature, man does not attempt to fight; he surrenders to her unconditionally. He drinks and drinks again from the intoxicating chalice that Siva fills to the brim with life and death; he drinks deep draughts of it, plunges into it, loses himself in it, abandons his being to it, and confesses, in transports of somber desperation, that God is all and all is God, that he himself is but an accident, a fleeting emanation of that unique substance. Or else, by means of a proud and patient immobility, he denies the existence of that hostile nature and avenges himself by logic on the reality that obliterates him.

Or, again, he flees westward and, approaching Persia, begins the long journey and the progressive unfettering of human liberty.

"In Persia," the young Cyrus says in Xenophon, "winter and summer are present at the same time." A light, dry atmosphere clears the head of the thick vapors that dull it in India. The land, arid on the surface, conceals in its bosom a thousand bubbling springs that seem to cry out for agricultural activity. Liberty awakens here and makes its presence known by a hatred of the previous state: the gods of India become *dives*, demonic forces; the sacred images are now considered idols: no more statues, no more art. Thus the iconoclastic genius of the heroic peoples presents itself at its wellspring. A multifarious divinity that prostituted spirit to matter in a confusion of infinite forms, the impious sanctity of a god-world, is succeeded by a dualism of light—pure, intelligent light and unclean, corporeal light. The former must prevail and its victory is the designated end for man and for the world. Since religion addresses itself to the interior man, the priesthood appears only to show its powerlessness. Every year the adherents of magism celebrate the massacre of the magi. Here we no longer find the passivity of the Indian, who can avenge his oppression only by killing himself before the very eyes of his oppressor.

Persia is the beginning of liberty within fatality. Here religion chooses its gods from a less material nature, but still from nature. These gods are: light, fire, celestial fire, and the sun. Azerbaidjan is the land of fire. The fecund and homicidal heat of the Caspian shores reminds us of India, which we thought we had escaped. A sense of universal instability gives the Persian an indifference that hampers his natural activity. Persia is the great highway of human kind; the Tartars on one side, the Arabs on the other, all the peoples of Asia have stopped, each in turn, in this caravanserai. Thus the men of this land have hardly troubled to erect any solid structures. In modern Isfahan, as in ancient Babylon, one builds with mud brick. The houses are lightly constructed kiosks, elegant pavilions, forms of tent raised in transit. One does not live in one's father's tent; everyone builds his own, and it dies when he does. One does not even save food for the morrow; what remains at evening is given to the poor. Thus human activity, at its first stirring, subsides again in discouragement and expires in indifference. Man seeks self-forgetfulness in intoxication. Not, as in India, in the intoxication of nature. Intoxication here is voluntary. In cold opium the Persian finds the dreams of a fantastical life and, ultimately, the repose of death.

Human liberty, which does not die, pursues its unfettering from Egypt to Judea, as it did from India to Persia. *Egypt is the gift of the Nile.* This is the river that carried from Ethiopia not only men and civilization, but also earth itself. In the sixteenth century the great Albuquerque conceived a plan to destroy Egypt. It would suffice to turn the Nile and make it empty into the Red Sea. Soon enough the sand of the desert would have buried the entire country. Every summer the river, descending from unknown mountains, comes to provide the year's subsistence. Anyone witnessing this precarious wonder, on which his very life depended, was already vanquished by nature. Generative power, fecundity, almighty Isis ruled his mind and kept him bent over his furrow. Nonetheless, liberty found a way to emerge. Egypt, like India, connected it to the dogma of the immortality of the soul. Human personality, rejected by this world, seized upon the other. Sometimes, even in this life, it rose against the tyranny of the gods. The brothers Cheops and Chephrem, who forbade sacrifices and were denounced by the priests, are thought to have been the founders of the pyramids, those tombs that were intended to eclipse all the temples. Thus the greatest monument of Egypt, that world of fatality, is the protest of humanity.

But human liberty did not rest in its flight until it reached the mountains of Judea. It sacrificed *the meat and onions* of Egypt and left its fertile valley for the rocky outcroppings of Cedron and the sandy shores of the Dead Sea. It cursed the golden calf of Egypt as Persia had shattered the idols of India. One god, one temple. Judges, then kings, take precedence over the priest. Eli and Samuel try to institute a priestly reign and fail. The leaders of the people are the strongmen who free it from the foreigner: a Gideon and his three hundred; an Aod, who fights with his two hands; a Samson, who carries away the city gates of his enemies on his shoulders; a David, who does not hesitate to eat the loaves of proposition. And then, alongside the heroic genius, the priest sees human liberty raise an even more formidable enemy from within the very order of religious things: seers, prophets arise among the people and communicate with God without passing by way of the temple. Among the Persians, nature prolonged her reign, not without struggle, within religion; among the Jews, she is dethroned. Light itself becomes shadow at the advent of the spirit; duality gives way to unity. For this little world of unity and spirit, a tiny spot of space between the mountains and the deserts is enough. It has been placed in the East only to condemn the East. With equal horror, it hears the lubricious chants of Astarte and the growls of Moloch echoing over rugged Libanon. Let the wandering horde of Araby, rootless and lawless, come out of the south: Israel recognizes Ismael as his brother but does not extend his hand. Let the foreigner perish: the holy city will not open her gates. She is content to keep in her tabernacle the priceless store of unity that the world will return to request of her on bended knee after it has begun, with Greece and Rome, its great work in the West.

If, in the realm of natural history, the animals of a superior order, man and the quadrupeds, are the most *articulated,*the most capable of the various motions that their activity stamps on them, if, among languages, those are best that respond by the variety of their inflections, the richness of their turns of phrase, the suppleness of their forms to the infinite requirements of intelligence, shall we not conclude that in geography, too, certain countries have been designed according to a more fortunate plan: better chiseled into gulfs and ports, better bounded by seas and mountains, better laced by valleys and rivers, better *articulated,* if I may use that term, which is to say, more capable of accomplishing all that liberty will want to derive from them. If you compare our little Europe with shapeless, massive Asia, how much more aptitude for movement does she not announce to the observing eye? Even in their common traits, Europe has the advantage. Both continents have three peninsulas to the south: the chunky square of Spain and that of Araby; the long spine of Italy and that of Hindustan, each with a great river in the north and an island to the south; finally, the swarm of isles and peninsulas, here called Greece and there, the second India. But gloomy Asia looks out upon the ocean, upon endlessness; she seems to be expecting of the South Pole a continent that does not yet exist. The peninsulas that Europe projects to the south are arms extended toward Africa, while to the north she girds her loins, like a mighty athlete, with Scandinavia and England. Her head belongs to France and her feet plunge down into the fecund barbarism of Asia. Note the powerful sinews on this marvelous body, extending from the Alps to the Pyrenees, and to the Carpathians and the Haimos, and the imperceptible marvel that is Greece in all the jostling variety of her hills and torrents, her capes and gulfs, in the multiplicity of her curves and angles, so vividly and cleverly set off. Consider her against the motionless straight line of unvarying Egypt: she twitches and flickers there on the map, a true symbol of mobility in our mobile West.

Europe is free soil: the slave who alights here is released from bondage, as was humanity, in flight from Asia. In the stern world of the West, nature gives nothing spontaneously; she imposes the exercise of liberty as ineluctable law. Therefore it was necessary to close ranks against the enemy and form the tight association that is *the city.*

This little world, enclosed by walls, drew the family and humanity into its artful unity. It set itself up in an eternal war against whatever persisted of the natural life of the eastern tribe. The form in which the Pelasgians had perpetuated Asia in Europe was obliterated by Athens and by Rome.

In this contest the three great moments of Greece define themselves: she attacks Asia in the Trojan War, repulses Asia at Salamis, and masters Asia with Alexander. But she masters Asia even better within herself and within the very walls of the city. She masters Asia when, with polygamy, she represses the sensuality of nature, which had maintained itself even in Judea, and declares woman to be the helpmate of man. She masters Asia when she reduces its gigantic idols to human scale and in so doing renders them capable of beauty and perfection. The gods reluctantly let themselves be drawn out of the gloomy sanctuary of India and of Egypt, to live in the light of day and on the public square. They descend from their majestic symbolism and take on common concerns. Until then they had contained the state within their immensity. In Greece they must become citizens, quit unbounded space and adopt a place, a country, make themselves small so as to fit within the city. These are the Dorian gods, those the Ionian; they are classed by the name of their worshipers. But, in recompense, see how they prosper among the people, how they follow in the rapid progress of humanity. The Pallas of the Iliad is a bloodthirsty, savage goddess who fights with Mars and wounds him with a stone. In the Odyssey she is the very voice of order and reason, interceding with the father of the gods in behalf of man.

What made Greece beautiful among beauteous things is this: placed at the midpoint where the divine is still divine and yet already human, where, working itself free of fatal nature, the flower of liberty opens into bloom, Greece has remained for the world the very type of the moment of beauty, of a beauty physical and still motionless, for Greek art hardly went beyond statuary. In literature this moment is that of Herodotos, of Plato and Sophocles; a brief moment, irrecoverable, which the manly wisdom of humankind cannot mourn, but which returns in memory with all the charm of first love.

In its very beauty this little world carries the seeds of its destruction. Beauty must fade; the grace of youth must give way to maturity; the child must become a man. Once Aristotle has clarified Greek learning, reduced it to prose, and codified it, once Alexander has spread Greece from the Hellespont to the Indus, it is all over. The son of Philip dreamed that all the world was a city and *his phalanx its citadel*. The Greek city is too constricted for that dream to come true; this requires a wider world, a world that brings together the character of both the tribe and the city. The fickle gods of Greece must take on greater gravity; they must emerge from art, which keeps them captive in matter, and free themselves from homeric Destiny, which keeps them under the heavy hand of Asia. Woman must leave the women's quarters and be effectively delivered from servitude. Atop the ruins of a Greek world carried wide and then destroyed lies its indestructible element, its atom, by which we will judge it, as one classes a shattered crystal by its last node. This node is the individual as conceived by Stoicism: self-collected, self-reliant, requiring nothing of the gods, accusing them of nothing, not even deigning to deny them.

The world of Greece was pure struggle: struggle against Asia, struggle within Greece itself, contest of the Ionians and the Dorians, of Sparta and Athens. Greece has two cities: that is to say, here the city is incomplete. Great Rome encloses the two cities, the two races within her walls: Etruscan and Latin, sacerdotal and heroic, eastern and western, patrician and plebeian, real property and movable property, stability and progress, nature and liberty.

Here the family reappears within the city; the domestic hearth of the Pelasgians is lit again on the altar of Vesta. The dualism of Persia returns, but it has passed from gods to men, from abstraction to reality, from religious metaphysics to civil law. The presence of two races within the same walls, their opposed interests, the need for equilibrium mark the beginning of that legal war before a judge whose formal qualities are the subject of jurisprudence. The warrior heroism of Persia and of Greece, that youthful love of combat, now becomes more temperate and consents to use no weapon within the city other than words. In this single combat fought with words, as in a war of conquest, the adversaries are eternally the one who *possesses* and the one who *demands*. The one has on his side authority, precedence, and written law; his feet rest securely on the ground in which he is rooted. The other, an athlete in motion, is armed with interpretation; time is on his side. The task of the judge, swept along by time, will be precisely to save the frozen letter by infusing it with spirit, perpetually renewed. Thus does liberty match wits with fatality and the law advance toward greater humaneness through ambiguity.

Rome is not an exclusive world. Within its walls, the city opens more and more to plebeians; without, it opens to Latium, to Italy, and to all the provinces. Just as the Roman family grows by adoption, extends itself, and divides by emancipation, the city adopts citizens, then entire towns under the name *municipes*, even while it propagates itself endlessly in its colonies: on each conquest it sets down a young Rome that represents the metropole.

Thus, whereas the Greek city, colonizing but never adopting, scattered itself abroad and was bound to die of exhaustion in the long run, Rome expands and contracts with the regularity of a living organism. She breathes in, if I may use the expression, the Latin, Sabine, and Etruscan peoples, they become Romans, and she breathes them out into her colonies.

In this fashion she assimilated the whole world. Western barbarism—Spain, Britain and Gaul—eastern civilization—Greece, Egypt, Asia, Syria—all in turn were caught in the current. The Semitic world resisted. Carthage was demolished, Judea thrown to the winds. All the rest were raised, despite themselves, to the level of uniform language, law, and religion. All became, willingly or not, Italians, Romans, senators, emperors. The Flavians, coming after the Caesars, who were Romans and patricians, are only Italians; the Antonines are Spaniards or Gauls; then the East asserts its rights against the West, and the African and Syrian emperors appear: Septimus, Caracalla, Heliogabalus, Alexander Severus; finally the provincials of the center: the tough peasants of Illyria, the Aurelians, the Probuses; barbarians even, Philip the Arab, Maximinus the Goth. Even before the empire was invaded, the imperial purple had been conquered by all nations.

This magnificent adoption of the peoples long led the Romans to believe that they had accomplished the great work of humanity. *Capitoli immobile saxum ... res romanae, perituraque regna...* Like Alexander, Rome deceived herself. She thought she was realizing the universal, the eternal city. And all the while the barbarians, the Christians, the slaves were protesting, each in their own way, that Rome was not the city of the world, and in different ways they pulled that factitious unity apart.

The heroic world of Greece and Rome, leaving all handicrafts to those whom they had conquered, to the slaves, did not pursue very far that victory of man over nature that we call industry. The old industrial races, the Pelasgians and other tribes, were reduced to servitude and perished. Then among the conquerors themselves the lower tribes perished, the Achaians, etc. And among the conquerors of the conquerors—Dorians, Ionians, Romans—the poor perished in their turn. He who has will have more; he who has little will have less and less, if industry does not throw a bridge across the gap that separates rich and poor. The economy caused the work of slaves, that is to say, of chattels, to be preferred to the work of men. The economy caused these chattels to be treated like chattels: if they perished, the master bought more, at a good price, and at a profit. The Syrians, Bithynians, Thracians, Germans, and Gauls long provisioned the greedy and murderous landscapes of Greece and Italy. All the while, the cancer of slavery was gaining ground and before long it could no longer be fed. Whereupon depopulation set in, preparing a place for the barbarians, who would come soon and willingly to the marketplaces of Rome—but as free men, and armed—to avenge their ancestors.

Long before this material, definitive dissolution of the empire, a powerful moral dissolution was at work on it internally. Greece and the East, which Rome thought she had subjugated, had invaded Rome instead and subjected her. From the time of the wars of Philip and Antiochos, the elegant gods of Athens had been finding their way into the Roman temples, under the names of the ancient Latin divinities, and occupying the altars of the conqueror gods. The Roman barbarian took up the study of Greece. He adopted its language, imitated its literature, reread the *Phaido* at Utica, died at Philippi reciting Euripides, and cried out in Greek under the blows of Brutus's dagger. The literary manifestation of this hellenized Rome is the Augustan Age; its fruit was Marcus Aurelius, the ideal of antique morality.

Behind Greece, the eastern world, having melded with Greece at Alexandria, was advancing toward that intellectual conquest of Rome. The translation of the empire into the East, brought about by Constantine, had been attempted early by Antony. He aimed to turn an eastern city into the capital of the world. Cleopatra swore: By the laws that I shall promulgate in the Capitol. For her to keep her word, the East would first have to conquer the West by the power of ideas. Alexandria was at least the center of that world inimical to Rome, the hearth on which all the beliefs, all the philosophies of Asia and of Europe simmered, the Rome of the intellectual world.

These beliefs, these religions did not gain easy entry into Rome. In rejecting the bacchanals, a horrified Rome had repulsed the first manifestation of the orgiastic cult of nature. But then a moment later, the painted priests of Cybele lead in the lion of the good goddess, amazing the people by their frenzied dances, their revolting trappings, lacerating their arms and legs and laughing at their wounds. Their god is ambiguous Atis, whose death and resurrection they celebrate by laughter and by tears. Then comes gloomy Serapis, yet another god of life and death. All the while, below the Capitol, beneath the very throne of Jupiter, gory Mithras is hollowing out a subterranean chapel, regenerating the man who thirsts for expiation in the filthy bath of the horrible bull sacrifice. Finally, a sect that emerged among the Jews, and that they rejected, also celebrates death and life; its God was executed like a slave. Tacitus does not know what to make of this new company. His sole acquaintance with the Christians is that he saw the festivals and gardens of Nero lit by the light of their burning corpses.

The difference between Christianity and the other eastern religions of life and death was, however, profound. These plunged man into matter; they took as their symbol the obscene sign of life and generation. Christianity embraced the spirit, embraced death, and adopted its funereal sign. Life, nature, matter, fatality were immolated. The body and the flesh, sanctified until then, were marked in its very temples by the sign of what consumes them: with horror one saw the worm that was gnawing them on the altar. Liberty, famished for pain, rushed to the amphitheater and relished being put to death.

I have gladly kissed the wooden cross that stands upright in the middle of the Coliseum, vanquished by it. How the young Christian faith must have embraced it as it entered among the lions and the leopards in that arena! Even today, whatever the future may bring, is that cross, more solitary with each passing day, not still the sole refuge of the religious soul? The altar has lost its place of honor, humanity slowly withdraws from it; but I ask you, oh, tell me if you know: has any other altar been erected?

In the arena of the Coliseum, the Christian and the barbarian meet, representing liberty for the East and for the West. We were born of their union, we and all the future.

"I see before me the gladiator lie/… And his droop'd head sinks gradually low/ … The arena swims around him—he is gone,/ Ere ceased the inhuman shout… / He heard it, but… his eyes… his heart [were] far away/… where his rude hut by the Danube lay/… his young barbarians all at play/… and their… mother… He… / Butchered to make Rome a holiday/… Shall he expire,/ And unavenged! —Arise! ye Goths…!"[1] May the Empire crumble and the circus, and that city drunk with blood!

Alaric protested that a fatal impetus was driving him against Rome. He sacked it and died. The arrière-ban of the barbarians—Goths, Burgundians, Heruli—revered the mysterious majesty of the city that no one violated unpunished. Even the man who boasted that no grass grew where his

---

1   Michelet translates the passage from *Childe Harold* rather freely into French. It appears more fully, in the original English, in the Notes and Clarifications. [Tr.]

horse had passed wheeled about and left Italy. The first barbarians were either intimidated or seduced by the city they were coming to destroy. They made terms with the Roman genius and retained the institution of slavery. It was not their task to restore the world.

Then came the Franks,[1] children of Odin, raging for pillage and warfare, craving wounds and death as others crave festivals and banquets, impatient to go drink beer from the skulls of their enemies in Walhalla. That sort went into battle nearly naked, leaped into a bark to round the Ocean, from the Bosporos to Batavia. Under their savage and pitiless rule domestic slavery nonetheless disappeared; it was followed by serfdom, itself a deliverance for oppressed humanity.

These barbarians brought a virginal nature to the Church. And the Church captured them. The Goths and the Burgundians, who saw in Jesus only a man, had received from Christianity neither its poetry nor its powerful unity. The Frank adopted the God-man, adopted a purified Rome, and took the name of Caesar. The swirling chaos of barbarism, which had sought to come to rest and become one since the time of Attila and of Theodoric, found its center in Charlemagne.

This unity, material and deceptive still, lasted one lifetime; falling into ruin, it left behind to rule Europe an episcopal aristocracy and a feudal aristocracy, crowned by pope and emperor respectively. A marvelous system in which the empire of God and the empire of man organized themselves and took up position face to face. In the feudal organization: material might, the flesh, and heredity; in the Church: the word, the spirit, and election. Might on every side, spirit at the center, spirit dominating might. Men of iron bent their rigid armor before an invisible sword; the son of a serf could put his foot on the neck of Frederick Barbarossa. Not only did the spirit dominate might; it swept might along in its train. The world of might, subjugated by the spirit, expressed itself in the crusades, a war of Europe against Asia, a war of sacred liberty against sensual and impious nature. For immediate purposes, however, it needed a material symbol of this opposition; that was the deliverance of the sepulcher of Jesus Christ. Everyone, men and women, young and old, set out, without arms, without provisions, without vessels, quite sure that God would feed them, defend them, and carry them over the seas. And little children, too, a contemporary

---

1   The ideas about the character of the Franks that follow here have been modified slightly by the author in his other works. He also found it desirable to explain the theory *on Satan* expounded below.

reports, followed in carriages and in their simplicity asked as they caught sight of the walls of every city, "Isn't that Jerusalem?"

Thus the long miracle of the Middle Ages accomplished itself over the term of a thousand years, that marvelous legend whose traces vanish daily from the face of the earth and which one would have doubted in a few centuries had it not fixed itself, crystallized itself for all eternity in the steeples, the spires, and the rose windows, in the countless arches of the cathedrals of Cologne and Strasbourg, in the five thousand marble statues that crown the cathedral of Milan. In contemplating this silent army of apostles and prophets, of saints and doctors rising in echelons from earth to heaven, who will not recognize the City of God raising men's minds up to Him? Each of those spires leaping upward is a prayer, an impotent vow stopped in its flight by the tyranny of matter. The steeple, shooting into the sky with such prodigious lift, protests before the Most High that at least there has been no want of will. All around, the fatal world of paganism growls and grimaces in the mongrel faces of a thousand hideous beasts, while at their feet barbarian warriors stand frozen in the attitude in which the spell of the Christian Word has caught them. In all eternity they will not recover themselves.

But the spell has been broken for humankind at large. The ultimate expression of Christianity in art, the Cologne cathedral, was broken off unfinished. Those immense naves proved too narrow for the invading multitude. A man in black arose among the people, a legist against the priestly alb, to oppose law with law. The shopkeeper came out of his dark shop to sound the communal alarm and bar his little winding street to the man on horseback. And then the man (was it a man?) who lived on all fours on his little patch of ground stood erect with a terrible laugh and struck the noble lord and his magnificent charger dead with a leveling ball, right through their useless armor.

Liberty has prevailed; justice has prevailed. The world of fatality has crumbled to dust. Spiritual power itself had set aside its title by invoking the protection of material might. The advancing triumph of the *self*, the age-old work of unfettering man, begun with the profanation of the tree of knowledge, has resumed. The world's heroic principle, liberty, long accursed and confounded with fatality under the name *Satan*, has appeared under its true name. Little by little, man has broken with the natural world of Asia and by industry and examination has fashioned a world sprung from liberty. He has removed himself from the nature-god of fatality, an exclusive divinity and treacherous mother who chose among her children, to reach the pure god, the god of the soul, who does not distinguish man from man and opens to all, in society, in religion, the parity of love and of the father's bosom.

***

How was the task of unfettering humankind accomplished in Europe? In what proportion did each of the political personages that are called states—France, Italy, England, and Germany—contribute to it?

Since the age of Greece and Rome, the world has lost the visible unity that gives the history of antiquity so simple and dramatic a character. Modern Europe is an organism of great complexity whose unity, whose heart and soul, lies not in one preponderant party or another, but rather in the relations among these parties and in how they are arranged with respect to one another in their deep meshing, in their innermost harmony. We cannot say what France has done, what she is and will be without addressing these questions to the assembled whole of the European world. France can only be explained by what surrounds her. Her personality can be grasped only by one who knows the other states that characterize her by their opposition.

The world of civilization is guarded at its two gates, toward Africa and toward Asia, by the Spanish and the Slavs, both sworn to an eternal crusade, Christian barbarians against Muslim barbarism. This world has as its two poles, north and south, Italy and Scandinavia. The fatality of race and climate weighs heavily on these extreme points.

At the center sprawls Germany the ill-defined. Like the Oder and the Waal, those vagrant rivers that set her limits so badly to east and west, Germany, too, has changed her banks one hundred times, both toward Poland and toward France. One need only follow, if one can, the capricious meanderings that the German language traces in Prussia and in Silesia, in Switzerland and in Lorraine, and in the Low Countries. As for the people, we find them everywhere. Germany has given her Swabians to Switzerland and to Sweden, her Goths to Spain, her Lombards to Lombardy, her Anglo-Saxons to England, her Franks to France. She has named and renewed all the populations of Europe. Language and people—this fecund stream has flowed and penetrated everywhere.

Even today, long after the time of the great migrations, the German loves to go abroad and to receive the foreigner at home. He is the most hospitable of men. Go in beneath that steeply sloping roof, into that ugly house of painted timbers, boldly take your place near the fire; never fear: you are obliging your host. Such is the partiality of the Germans for the foreigner. The Austrian, the Swabian, so maltreated by our troops, often wept at the departure of the French. In any smoky hovel you will find all the newspapers of France. The German has a feeling for the world; he loves and adopts the fashions and the ideas of other peoples; but he reserves the right to speak ill of them.

The characteristic mark of this race, which was to mix with so many others, is easy self-abnegation. The vassal gives himself to his lord; the student and the artisan give themselves to their corporations. In these associations, self-interest is secondary; the essential thing is a gathering of friends, mutual help, and those rites, symbols, and initiations that are a religion of choice for the members. The communal table is an altar on which the German makes a sacrifice of egoism; one man surrenders his heart to another, and his dignity and reason to the pleasures of the senses. Laughable, touching mysteries of old Germany: baptism by beer, sacred symbolism of smiths and masons, solemn initiations of coopers and carpenters. Little enough remains of all this, but in that little, one still finds that sympathetic, disinterested spirit.

No surprise then that in Germany we first see a man make himself the liege of another, put his hands into the hands of the other and vow to die for him. This selfless, unconditional devotion, which the peoples of the south find so laughable, has nonetheless been the grandeur of the Germanic race. This is how the ancient bands that conquered the Empire, gathered each around a chief, founded the modern monarchies. They gave their lives to this chief of their choosing; they gave him their very glory. In the ancient German lays all the exploits of the nation are attributed to a handful of heroes. In the chief is concentrated the honor of the people, of which he becomes the colossal type. Might, beauty, grandeur, all the noble feats of arms are massed in Siegfried, Dietrich, Frederick Barbarossa, in Rudolf of Hapsburg. Their faithful companions kept back nothing for themselves.

Above the lord, above the counts and dukes, and the electors and the Emperor, at the very apex of the hierarchy, Germany has placed woman

(*Frau*). *Velleda*, says Tacitus, *was worshiped in her lifetime*. An ancient minnesinger places woman on *a throne, with twelve stars for a crown and a man's head for her footstool*. If poetry is anywhere an affair of the heart, it is here. The minnelieder are full of infantine tears, of that abandoned suffering which is a sorrow to itself and can no longer find expression. Here you will find neither *jongleurs*, nor *gai savoir*, even less the frivolous dialectics of the *cours d'amour*. The object of these lays is ideal woman, the Virgin, who makes them forget God and the saints. It is all greensward and flowers; this last they never exhaust. This poetry, childlike and profound at once, lets itself be led by the magnetic attraction of nature, which it will deify in the end. The German genius, an admirable mixture of force and of childhood, comes before me in the figure of Wolfram's Parsifal, that mighty knight whom the care of a timid mother has kept in the innocence and touching ignorance of first youth. He escapes and finds his way through forests and wildernesses to the city of miracles. But a wounded bird stains the snow with three drops of blood, and the hero sees in these colors the rose and white of his one true love. He stops, lost in a dream, contemplating in present reality the ideal that fills his mind. Woe betide any who try to put an end to the dream; without budging from the spot, he unhorses the knights who come one after another to rip him from his reverie.

Thus does the abnegation and profound disinterestedness of the German genius first burst forth in feudal devotion, in love and poetry. Deceived by the finite, it addresses itself to the infinite. Having sacrificed itself to its lord and its lady, what will it refuse its God? Nothing, not even its morality, its liberty. It will throw everything into that abyss; it will melt man into the universe and the universe into God. Having been prepared by Protestant mysticism, it will have no difficultly adopting Schelling's pantheism, and the adultery of matter and spirit will be consummated anew. Dear God, where do we now find ourselves? We have been plunged back into India. Could we then have made this long journey in vain? At this point the universal sympathy, or the universal indifference, of the German genius manifests itself, with its immoral consequences. All religion, all philosophy, all history, whatever comes—the author of *Faust*, the Faust of our own time, will reflect them, will absorb them into the ocean of his poetry.

Yes, Germany is India in Europe, vast, vague, shifting, and fecund, like her God, the Proteus of pantheism. As long as the Indo-Germanic tribe was not contained and shut in by the strong barriers of surrounding monarchies, it spilled over, spread out over Europe, which it changed as it, too, was changed. Left at the time to its natural mobility, the tribe knew neither walls nor towns. "Every family," says Tacitus, "stops where it will, in a wood, on a meadow, by a spring." But as the floodtide of another barbarism, of Slavs, Avars, and Hungarians, was rising in the rear, and France to the west was closing up, the Germans had to press together in order not to lose their footing, had to build strongholds, *invent* towns. They had to pledge themselves to dukes and counts, gather themselves into circles, into provinces. Tossed down in the middle of Europe as a battleground for all wars, Germany attached herself, for good or ill, to feudalism and remained barbarian in order not to perish. This is what explains the marvelous spectacle of a race forever young and virginal, which one sees engaged as if by magic in a transparent civilization, the way liquid caught up quickly remains fluid at the center of a faulty crystal. Hence the bizarre contrasts that make Germany into a land of monstrous diversity. Some states of twenty million souls, others of twenty thousand. An infinite splintering, an infinitely varied law of feudal lordships; and, alongside, a grand monarchy disciplined like a regiment. Towns built yesterday, all in white, leveled, aligned, drawn at right angles, tedious, sullen little Londons. Others, like our good Nuremberg, where the houses, grotesquely painted, still preach the gospel to passersby; or, to bring together all these contrasts, learned libraries in the middle of the forest, and stags coming to drink under the balconies of electors. These surface contrasts only express oppositions of custom. The slavery of serfdom, and free medieval communes: everything is to be found in this curious museum, where every step in space is also a journey in time. In many provinces, woman is a servant, as she was the servant of the barbarian warrior, which does not prevent her being deified by the ideal genius of chivalry.

The strongest of all these contradictions is the one that keeps a people open to innovation and enamored of foreign things even under the yoke of the Middle Ages. So little tenacity and yet such permanence of usage and custom! What Germany lacks is surely not desire for change, for independence. How many times has she not risen, only to fall back again soon after. The ancient Saxon genius, Germany's eternal political opposition, the fierce pride of the Scandinavian tribes, the whole North protests against the pantheistic bent of the southern provinces. It refuses to lose its personality in a man, in God, or in nature. This attitude of the North displays itself with magnificent ostentation. In Iceland the gods will die like us. Man was here before them; the universe was carved from the limbs of a giant. *Who do you believe in?* Saint Olaf asked one of his warriors. *I believe in myself,* the man replied. How is it then that this proud genius always falls back so quickly, in religion into mysticism, in politics into despotism? Sweden, champion of Protestant freedom under Gustavus-Adolfus, submitted to the Rosicrucians. Who spoke louder than Luther against the tyranny of Rome—only to destroy the doctrine of free will? In Luther's lifetime, at his very table, began the mysticism that would triumph in Boehme. Kant inscribed on his standard: Critique and Liberty. Germany intended to be strong and free at last—and for safety's sake, she locked herself into the shackles of a terrible formalism. But this inconstant nature always slipped free, by means of art and feeling, by means of Goethe and Jacobi. Then came Fichte, that inflexible stoic and ardent patriot. To liberate mankind he resorted to the sole remaining means: he did away with the world, just as he would have liked to deliver Germany by doing away with France. Vain hopes of mere men! Fichte's philosophy, Koerner's songs, 1814: all ended in sleep, a troubled sleep, no doubt. Germany let herself be lulled back to sleep with the pantheism of Schelling, and if the North escaped by means of Hegel, it was only to violate the sacred refuge of human liberty, to turn history to stone. In their hands, the social world became a god, a frozen god, a god without feeling, wholly suited to console and prolong the national lethargy.

No indeed. Great Germany, learned and powerful Germany has no right to despise little Italy, which she overwhelms. Italy at least can plead the languor of the climate, the disproportionate forces of the conquerors, her long disorganization. Give her time, this ancient mistress of the world, this old rival of Germania. What caused the humiliation of Italy as a people, what subjected her to mild, easily disciplined Germany is precisely the indomitable personality, the undisciplinable originality that keeps individuals apart in Italy.

The instinct for abnegation that we found in Germany is foreign to Italy. In this respect, and in all others, the opposition between the two peoples is sharp. The Italian has no intention of abnegating himself, of losing himself, with God and the world, in one and the same idealism. He makes God come down to him, materializes him, forms him at his pleasure, and seeks here an objet d'art. He makes of religion, often in good faith, an object of government. Down through the ages, it appears to him under the aspect of practical utility. Etruscan divination was the art of ambushing the gods' knowledge of the interests of the world, it was part of politics and jurisprudence. The prayers and formulas of augury are veritable contracts with the gods. The augur looks for the most precise terms, never promises too much, undertakes nothing, takes precautions against the other party. He has no fear of taxing the gods with questions and new stipulations. To find the finest fruits, to recover a lost bird, one took the divining rod and traced the sacred lines.

Canon law, like the law of augury, pertained to the government of this world. We know how artfully the Roman church reached and regulated all human action, as the stuff of sin. Theology, for good or ill, was subsumed into jurisprudence; the popes were legists. "We here know the affairs of God better than you men of law," a king of France wrote them.

Italy alone had a civil architecture in the various eras when other nations knew only religious architecture. The word *pontifex* means builder of bridges. Etruscan monuments, different in this respect from those of the East, all have practical utility as their purpose. These are city walls, aqueducts, tombs; one hears less about Etruscan temples. Medieval Italy built many churches, but they were the venues of political assemblies. While Germany, England, and France were erecting only religious edifices, Italy was building roads and canals. Thus Germany surpassed Italy in the construction of her immense cathedrals. Gian Galeazzo Sforza was obliged to ask Strasbourg for architects to close the vaults of the Milan cathedral.

If Italian individuality does not give itself to God unconditionally, then how much less likely is it to give itself to man! You will find in medieval Italy more than one image of feudalism—heavy armor, mighty chargers, fortified castles—but never the very essence of feudalism, one man's pledged faith to another. Italian heroism is of a higher order. What care has it of a mortal man, a flesh that will perish, and a heart that will soon beat no more? It knows how to die (though it does not seek death), but to die for an idea. I know of a certain man in a certain fortress who amid the harshest trials will keep the secret of liberty to the death. In the eyes of the compatriots of Machiavelli, every other kind of devotion is simplemindedness, infantilism. Adventurous questing after useless perils, the deification of woman, the religion of fidelity, the dreamlike transports of a feudal world—all this excites their inextinguishable laughter. Their chivalric poem is the satire of chivalry, *Orlando Furioso*. They have no associations, neither industrial nor military, if not for a specific purpose, for an interest, an idea.

The Italian genius is passionate but stern, a stranger to vague sympathies. This is not the natural world of family and of tribe; it is the artificial world of the city. Confined by nature in the narrow valleys of the Apennines, isolated by rivers hard to navigate, it closes itself up yet again within walls. There it rules, far from nature, in marble palaces, where it lives on harmony, rhythm, and number. If it emerges, it is to build rock gardens for its *villas*. From the first it is characterized by the harmony of civil life, by legislation and by jurisprudence. After countless barbarian invasions, indestructible Roman law reappears at Bologna and throughout Italy. The subtleties of Tribonianus are made yet more subtle by Accursio and Bartolus of Sassoferrato. With the jurists, mathematicians return. Cardano and Tartaglia perpetuate Archytas and Pythagoras. Their abstract geometry is received into the concrete geometry of architecture, which is the art of the material city, as legislation is the art of the moral city. At Rome and Florence the human figure reproduces in painting the severity, sometimes the spareness of architecture. Only in the north, in the Venetian palette and in Lombard grace, does painting consent to humanize man. As to nature, it will rarely dare to show itself in painting: few landscapes, little descriptive poetry in Italy.

Poetry here takes its inspiration from the genius of the city. To be sure, this is a land where everyone sings; the climate loosens every tongue. But the true Italian poet is the architect of the invisible city whose symbolic circles are the setting of the *Divina Commedia*. Dante is the complete expression of the Italian idea of rhythm and number; he has measured, drawn, and sung his inferno. And it is in the harmonic form of the city that history and humanity appeared before the founder of the philosophy of history, the Dante of Italy's age of prose, Giambatista Vico. In the duality of *corso* and *ricorso*, in the threefold ages, in the geometric beauty of its form, the *Scienza nuova* represents for me the rhythmic beauty of Etruria and of pythagorean Greece.

Even when the Italian leaves the city, he takes its image with him and imprints it everywhere. We know with what strict exactitude Etruscan religion and Roman politics measured and mapped the open fields. The *agrimensor* and the haruspex followed after the conquering legions everywhere to cast the new colony on the sacred model of the metropole. Whereas among the German nations a man attaches himself to his plot of ground, puts down roots, and loves to take his name from his estate, the Italian gives it his. He sees there only one more connection with the city, only a matter of civil interest. The jurist and the military strategist will come to reconnoiter the territory and correct or shift the boundaries, to transfer or hold the property, according to the diverse means of their respective arts.

Italy is the mother of tactics as of jurisprudence. In the hands of the Italian *condottieri*—the Alberics, the Sforzas, and the Malatestas of Romagna, the Braccios, the Baglionis, and the Piccininos of Umbria—war became a science. Italy furnished the Levant with engineers. The founders of military architecture are Italians. The foremost captain of antiquity, Caesar, belongs to Italy; the foremost of modern times was a man of the Italian race adopted by France. If we knew nothing of Napoleon's origins, would not the character of his genius, poetic and practical at once, the austere beauty of his profile make us recognize the compatriot of Machiavelli and of Dante?

It is time to be done with those preposterous declamations on the weakness of the Italian character. Do you intend to judge the value of the Italians by the populace of Naples? You might just as well judge France by the *canuts* of Lyon. Let us leave it to English gentlemen and German poets to go seeking inspiration for their sublime contempt and large-minded rage at the tables of the Italians of Rome and Milan. Did they not also insult Greece in her tomb, on the very eve of her resurrection? Frivolous, cruel men who conflate Lazzaroni and Romagnoli, heroes and cowards under the same opprobrium, have you forgotten Bonaparte's Italian army and all the feats of arms of the Piedmontese? And just lately, did those whom you accused of not knowing how to draw their swords for their country not in fact know how to die for you?[1]

Italy has changed, we hear, and that is held to explain and justify her woes. But I maintain that no people has remained more like itself. I have already noted the continuity of the Italian genius from ancient to modern times. I will find it only too easy to trace that continuity in any number of less important details.

---

1   A considerable number of Italians were among the foreigners who fought for the freedom of France in the July days of 1830. The names of only a few have been recorded: "M. Giannone (the author of *L'Esule*) invariably showed up at the most dangerous spots; M. Bonnizzi was wounded in the left arm; M. Libri began the first day wielding a stick; on the second he seized a gun from a soldier; and on the third, he armed himself fully by disarming a high-ranking officer; M. Libri remained on the front line of our heroes for sixty hours." (See the newspaper *Le Temps* for 30 July until 1 August; see also the *Revue française* for November 1829).

The national costume is almost the same, at least among the people. I see the *venetus cucullus* everywhere, the long steel hairpins of the women, necklaces and rings like those recovered at Pompeii, even sandals and the *pileus* that you will find near Fondi.

The diet is comparable. In the towns, the same narrow streets. The *thermopoles*, now called cafés. The *prandium* at midday, the siesta, and the evening promenade. In every age, the same crowd gathered around the improviser, whether he is called Statius or Dante or Sgricci. In the *filosofi* of Venice, the open-air *literati*, we meet the Ennianistae of antiquity. Only, Ariosto and Tasso have taken the place of Ennius.

In the countryside, the same system of cultivation. The plow is the one that Virgil describes. In Tuscany the cattle are, as always, penned up and fed on foliage so that they will not damage the vines and the olive trees. In other parts, they still make their timeless journey from the hills to the plains of Rome and Puglia, and from the plain back to the hills.

Every province has remained true to its genius. Naples is still Greek, whatever the barbarians may have done. The savage type of the Bruttians is manifestly conserved in San Giovanni in Fiore. The Neapolitans are still noisy and big talkers. Naples is a city of lawyers. There have been musical contests at Naples since antiquity. The philosophical genius of Magna Graeca—does it not live again in Telesio, in Campanella, and in the unhappy Bruno?

In the south, idealism, speculation, and the Greeks; in the north, sensualism, action, and the Celts. Carpenters, joiners, peddlers, and masons come from Novarra, Como, and Bergamo. Bergamo, home of Harlequin, is also the home of the ancient comedian Caecilius Statius.

The same long continuity in the lands of the center, in Rome and Etruria. The cyclopean character of the walls of Volterra is no less striking in the edifices of Florence, in the massiveness of the Pitti Palace. The formal stiffness of Etruscan art reappears in Giotto and is visible still in Michelangelo. But I plan to demonstrate the sameness of Etruria down through the ages more completely elsewhere.

When barbarous Sulla had devastated Etruria, he chose a site in the valley of the Arno, founded a city there, and named it after the mysterious name of Rome. That name, known only to patricians, who were forbidden to pronounce it, was *Flora*. He called the new city *Florentia*. Florence responded to this augury. The poet of Italy's earliest times, the author of the *Aeneid*, came from the Etruscan colony of Mantua, and it is to a Tuscan, a Florentine, that we owe the poem of medieval times, the *Divine Comedy*. Italy is the land of traditions and of historical perpetuity. *Questa provincia,* said Machiavelli with his usual force and gravity, *pare nata a risuscitare le cose morte.*

At the center of the peninsula, the people is equally unchanged. These men were never given to art or to learning. Most of Rome's illustrious writers—Catullus, Virgil, Horace, Ovid, Lucan and Juvenal, Cicero, Livy, Seneca, and the Plinys—and any number of others less illustrious, came to Rome from elsewhere. The same in the Middle Ages. Her theologian and her artist are two foreigners, Saint Thomas of Aquino and Raphael of Urbino. To Rome, however, belong bitter, mordant satire and tragic laughter. Lucullus and Juvenal were native Romans; Salvatore Rosa and Monti were Romans by adoption.

The true vocation of the Roman was political action. Unable to go on acting, he falls to dreaming. Consider this monumental race in its streets and on the public square: you will be struck to see how proud it is. These are the bas-reliefs of Trajan's column, come down to earth and walking among us. Not for anything on earth would a Roman do servile labor. Men must come from the Abruzzi to bring in the harvest and mend the roads, from Bergamo to carry loads. His wife would disdain to darn her cloak; that requires a Jew. Rome's sole export is earth itself, rags, and antiquities.

As in the time when Juvenal shows us the praetor and the tribune collecting the *sportula* from door to door, the Roman of today begs nobly. His staple food is still pork. Butchers and sausage makers are almost the only shops in Rome. Sensual and cruel always, the Roman now contents himself with bullfights, for want of gladiators. Accuse him of ferocity, if you will, but not of weakness: his knife would answer for him. He is never without his knife. A knife thrust is a frequent, natural gesture in Rome. And one should see with what furious joy he fires his race horse on. His Carnival cry is bloody and leveling: *Death to my lord abbot, death to the beautiful princess!* he cries as loudly as he ever cried, "The Christians to the lions." Undeniably, the air of that city carries a whiff of something stormy, frenzied, and immoral. In the midst of the most stunning contrasts, among the monuments of every age—Egyptian, Etruscan, Greek, Roman—at the meeting place of all the races of the world, you hear every language but Italian; there are more foreigners than Romans, and kings among the crowd. One's head spins, vertigo sets in; I am not surprised that so many emperors, seeing all this whirling at their feet, went mad.

A more melancholy similarity between ancient times and modern is the emptiness of the environs of Rome and of the Italian countryside in general. Whatever the agricultural genius of the ancient Latins, one sees that from the time of the Republic a part of the countryside was left in meadowland (*prata Mucia, Quintia*, etc.). Cato recommends pasturage as the best use of land. That counsel was followed: it gave landlords dispensation not to live on their holdings or hire the poor; a handful of slaves was all they needed. Thus Rome went the way of England under Henry VIII, when it was said that *the sheep had eaten the people*. The desolation spread. Caesar already was charged with draining the Pontine Marshes. Strabo, Pliny, and Tacitus all complain of *mala aria*. And Lucan could say without exaggeration: *Urbs nos una capit*.

That note condemns Italy. The desert around Rome, as isolated on dry land as is Venice surrounded by water, presents the sorry symbol of the harm done by that city life (*urbanitas*) to which the Italian genius is given. In the Etruscan cities of antiquity and in the Guelph cities of the Middle Ages, Italy has twice seen industry emerge and cities come to dominate the countryside. And twice destructive industry—war—has risen against productive industry, devoured the countryside and emptied out the towns; war as wager and way of life; war feeding on itself: Rome in ancient times, the *condottieri* of the Middle Ages.

Poor Italy has changed little, and this is her undoing. She has constantly been subjected to the two-fold fatality of her climate and of a narrow, concentrating social system. That system has dried up and eaten out the heart of Italy (*Italum robur*), by which I mean Rome and ancient Samnium. From the time of Honorius, even the *smiling* Campagna had been abandoned and left uncultivated. It seemed for a time that the Germanic tribes, enemies of cities, would restore importance to the countrysides they divided among themselves. It was not to be. The men of the North melted like snow on this sunbaked ground. The Italian cities absorbed the Goths in less than a century. The Lombards, the most energetic race of Germany, did not hold out two hundred years. To judge by the looks of the people and by the language, the influence of the Germanic invasions was wholly superficial. The barbarians often believed they had conquered Italy; but they managed to introduce few Teutonic words into that indomitable idiom. In vain the German, or Ghibelline, party organized itself into feudal forms, erected castles on the hilltops, and armed the countrysides against the cities. The castles were destroyed, the countrysides absorbed by the towns, the towns isolated by depopulation of the countryside and leveled socially by the radicalism of the Roman church, of the Guelph faction, and of tyrants. With the Ghibelline aristocracy, they lost all military spirit, and the land found itself delivered over to foreigners. Since that time Italy's center of gravity, laid in Magna Graeca in the South during antiquity, has been shifted northward and lies today in Romagna, the Milanese, and Piedmont, the Celtic parts of Italy. It suffices to say that Italy now has little hope of originality and that she will look to France for a long time yet.

Thus fatality pursues us even into Europe, which liberty had seemed to reserve for itself. We have found it in tribal life and in city life, in Germany and in Italy. There as here, moral liberty is obstructed, blocked by local influences of race and climate. Equally, man here carries the mark of fatality in his aspect. The land is reflected in him, one would say as in a mirror. Germany entire is in the face of the German: pale blue eyes, like uncertain skies; fair hair or fawn, like the hind of the Odenwald. Even the passing years are not always adequate to mark his looks: from earliest youth into full maturity you will often observe the soft and undefined beauty of childhood. Thus man blends with the nature that surrounds him. The Italian seems more detached from it. His dark eyes and lively movements bespeak a strong personality, though that ardent eye wanders and falls to dreaming. His gaze is sometimes so mobile that it frightens; his hair, as black as the wines of the South, his deeply tanned complexion, point to the son of the vine and the sun and plunge him back into the fatality from which he had seemed set free.

These powerful local influences, which make a man one with his land, by attaching at least his heart and soul to his hillside, to his native valley, keep him in a state of isolation, of dispersion, and of mutual hostility. The ancient opposition of *Saxony and the Empire* stubbornly persists down through the ages. Each of the two halves, even, is less than homogeneous. The Hessian hates the Franconian; the Franconian, the Bavarian; the Bavarian, the Austrian. The Greek of Calabria and the Celt of Milan are no more removed from one another than are the son of rugged Samnium and the son of gentle Etruria. This diversity of provinces and towns expresses itself in mutual derision, in the creation of local comedy, in the opposition of Bergamesque Harlequin and Neapolitan Pulcinella, of Saxon Eulenspiegel and Austrian Hanswurst.

In such countries there will be a juxtaposition of diverse races, but never an intimate fusion. The crossing of races, the mixing of opposed civilizations is, however, liberty's most potent aid. The diverse fatalities that they bring to this mix cancel and neutralize each other. In Asia, especially before Islam, the races, isolated into tribes in diverse countrysides and ranked in hierarchies of caste in any given countryside, represent distinct ideas, hardly communicate, and keep to themselves. As we move westward, races and ideas, everything combines and becomes more complicated. The mix, imperfect in Italy and Germany, uneven in Spain and England, is even and perfect in France. That which is least simple, least natural, most artificial—which is to say, least fatal, most human, and most free in the world—is Europe; and that which is most European, is my homeland, is France.

Germany has no center; Italy has one no longer. France has a center; unified and the same for many centuries, she may be considered a living, breathing person. The sign and warrant of a living organism, the power to assimilate, is present here in the highest degree: French France has understood how to attract, absorb, and make one all the Frances that surrounded her: English, German, Spanish France. She has neutralized one by means of another and converted all into her substance. She has moderated Brittany with Normandy, the Franche-Comté with Burgundy, Guyenne and Gascony with Languedoc, Provence with Dauphiné. She has made the North more southerly, the South more northerly; to the South she has brought the chivalric genius of Normandy and Lorraine, to the North, the Roman form of Toulousian municipality, the Greek industrialism of Marseille.

The France that is French, the center of the monarchy, the basin of the Seine and of the Loire, is a remarkably flat land, pale and nondescript. When you drop down from the sublime peaks of the Alps, the harsh valleys of the Jura, the vine-covered slopes of Burgundy onto the monotone landscapes of Champagne and the Île de France, amid those muddy, meandering rivers, those towns of lime and timber, your spirits are seized by tedium and distaste. You will see plenty of rich countrysides, thriving farms and fine cattle. But that prosaic picture of ease and well-being would make you long for impoverished Switzerland and even for the desolation of the Roman campagna. As for the people, do not expect the quick retort of Gascony nor Provençal grace nor the sly, all-conquering prickliness of Normandy, even less the persistence of the Auvergnat and the obstinacy of the Breton. With due allowance for scale, our remote provinces are like Italy and southern Germany, like all lands broken up by mountains and steep valleys: the more isolated man, lacking the powerful support of division of labor and communication of ideas, is often more ingenious and more original, but also less practiced at comparing, less cultivated, less humanized, less *social*. The man of central France amounts to less as an individual, but there the mass of men is worth more. His particular genius lies precisely in what foreigners, even provincials call insignificance and indifference and what one should rather call a universal aptitude, capacity, and receptivity. It is the character of the center of France to present none of the originalities of the provinces, to participate in all and remain neutral, to borrow from each everything that does not exclude the others, to form the connection, the intermediary among all, to the point where each provincial quality can readily recognize in the intermediary its kinship with the rest. This is the superiority of central France over the provinces, of all France over Europe.

This intimate fusion of races is the very identity of our nation, its personality. Let us ask what composes the particular genius of this multiple unity, of this gigantic person composed of thirty million men.

This genius is action, and that is why the world belongs to it. This is a people composed of men of war and men of affairs, which amounts in many respects to the same thing. In the war of juridical subtleties, one has to say, we take first place, whether we should boast of it or not; the public prosecutor is a born Frenchman. Before legists entered affairs, theology and scholasticism were the means of access. Paris was then the capital of dialectics for Europe. Its University, truly universal, was divided into *nations*. The pick of excellence throughout the world came to exercise itself in this gymnastics. Around the chair of Duns Scotus stood Dante and Ramon Lull, an Italian and a Spaniard. From the teachings of a single professor there went forth two popes and fifty bishops. Here, as much as in the crusades or the English Wars, the nation's genius for battle flashed. Frightful mêlées of syllogisms were fought on the front lines of the two enemy camps—the Île and the Mount, the Parvis and Sainte-Geneviève, church and town, authority and liberty. From there knights errant of dialectics went out on expedition, like the terrible Abailard who unhorsed Guillaume de Champeaux and Anselm de Laon and threw down the glove at the Church in defying Saint Bernard.

A taste for war and action, a swift sword, argument and sophistry ever at the ready—these are the common characteristics of the Celtic peoples.

Hibernian valor and dialectic are no less celebrated than those of France. What is peculiarly French, what France has beyond all other peoples, is a social genius, with three characteristics in apparent contradiction: an easy acceptance of foreign ideas, an ardent proselytism that leads her to spread her ideas abroad, and a capacity for organization that sums up and codifies one and the other.

We know that France made herself Italian in the sixteenth century and English at the end of the eighteenth. Conversely, in the seventeenth century and in our own, she made other nations French. Action, reaction; absorption, resorption: the alternating motion of the true organism. But what is the nature of the action of France? This is what needs to be explained. The pretext of our wars is love of conquest, and in this we, too, are deceived. For proselytism is the more ardent motive. The Frenchman wants most of all to imprint his personality on the vanquished, not as his own, but as the type of the beautiful and the good; such is his simple conviction. He really believes that he can do nothing more useful for the world than to give it his ideas, his customs, and his fashions. He will convert other peoples to these things sword in hand, and after battle he will show them, half in vanity, half in sympathy, all that they stand to gain by becoming French. Do not laugh: one who tries steadfastly to make the world in his own image will succeed in the end. The English see only simplemindedness in these wars without conquest, in these efforts without material result. They do not understand that we fail at the petty end of an immediate interest only in order to attain a higher, grander one. The universal assimilation that France is moving toward is not at all the one dreamed of by England and Rome in their egotistical and materialist politics. It is, rather, an assimilation of minds, a conquering of wills: who to date has succeeded better here than we have done? Every one of our armies, withdrawing, has left behind a France. Our language reigns supreme in Europe; our literature invaded England under Charles II, Italy and Germany in the last century; today it is our laws, our liberty, strong and pure, that we are about to impart to the world. This is the way of France, in her ardent proselytism, in her appealing instinct for intellectual fecundation.

France eagerly imports, exports new ideas and with marvelous capacity melds one with the other in her crucible. She is the legislative people of modern times, as Rome was the legislative people of antiquity. Just as Rome received into her bosom the opposed legal systems of two different races, the Etruscan and the Latin, France in her ancient legislation was Germanic to the Loire and Roman south of that river. The French Revolution married the two elements in our *Code Civil*.

France acts and reasons, decrees and does battle; she shakes the world, makes history and recounts it. History is the recounting of action. Nowhere else will you find memoirs, individual histories, not in England, nor in Germany, nor in Italy. There are few exceptions. In medieval Italy, the life of a man was the life of the city. English hauteur is such that no personality will condescend to render an account of itself. The modest nature of the German does not permit him to attach that much importance to what he has been able to do. Read the hasty notes dictated by Goetz of the Iron Hand: how he admits his misadventures. Germany is more fit for epic than for history; she reserves glory for her ancient heroes and happily disdains the present. For France the present is everything. She seizes upon it with an alacrity all her own. As soon as someone has done something, seen something—quick—he writes it down. Often he exaggerates. One should see what-all *our men* do in the ancient chronicles. The French have long been accused of bragging. But in justice one must say that this spirit of exaggeration is often disinterested. It comes from a habitual desire to create an effect; in other words, it is the result of an oratorical, rhetorical genius, which is both a strength and a weakness of our national character.

Let us admit it: the literature of France is eloquence and rhetoric, just as her art is fashion—both equally intent on adorning, on exaggerating the personality. Rhetoric and eloquence, of which rhetoric is by turns the art and the abuse, speak to be heard by others; poetry, to be heard by itself. Eloquence can come to life only in society, in liberty. Nature weighs upon the poet. Poetry is the fatal echo of this, the sound made by a humanity struck by nature. Eloquence is the free voice of a man trying to bring the free will of his fellow man to common cognizance. This people is therefore, among all others, the people of rhetors and of prose writers.

France is the land of prose. What do all the prosaists of the world amount to beside Bossuet, Pascal, Montesquieu, and Voltaire? Now, when one says prose, one is speaking of the least figurative form, the least concrete, the most abstract, the most pure, the most transparent. Expressed differently, the least material, the most free, the most common to all men, the most *human*. Prose is the ultimate form of thought, is what is most removed from vague and inactive reverie, what is closest to action. The passage from mute symbolism to poetry and from poetry to prose is a progression toward an equality of enlightenment; it is a process of intellectual leveling. Thus from the mysterious hierarchy of eastern caste heroic aristocracy emerges; and from heroic aristocracy, modern democracy. Nowhere can the democratic genius of our nation be better seen than in its eminently prosaic character, and this is how she is destined to raise all thinking beings to a level of equality.

The democratic genius of France is no recent thing. It is visible — confused and obscure but no less real — from the earliest origins of our history. It grew for a long time, sheltered by and even taking the form of religious power. Before the Romans, before Caesar, I see the Gallic priest, the rival of the clan chieftains, arise, not by right of birth and flesh, but through initiation, that is to say, through the spirit, equality. The Druids, coming from the people, ally themselves with the people of the towns, against the aristocracy. After the barbarian invasions, after the introduction of feudalism, the Roman, the vanquished — which is to say, the people — is represented by the priest, who is elected from the people: a man of the spirit, against the man of landholding and of force. The latter, rooted, localized within his fief and for this very reason scattered about the territory, tends toward isolation, toward barbarism. The priest, like the serf, the class to which he often belongs, looks to central power, which is royal. Abstract, divine right of the king and of the priest; concrete, human right of the baron embedded in his land. The close association of the first two is characteristic of the most popular kings of each of the three races: good king Dagobert, Louis le Bon or le Débonnaire, good king Robert, and finally Saint Louis. The type of the king of France is the saint. The priest and, no less, the king favor the freeing of the serfs; every man who escapes the local servitude of the soil belongs to them, to central power, abstract and of the spirit. Priests and kings then contrive to free entire towns, to create communes and to gather there an anti-feudal army. Now the people, which until then reached liberty only in the person of the priest, appears for the first time in its own proper form.

But priest and monarch soon rued having roused the turbulent freedom of the communes, a freedom that was turning against them. The kings put a stop to the rapid emigration of laborers, who were fleeing the land to take refuge behind the walls of the towns. In so doing, they delayed the fall of feudalism. Feudalism would have to perish, but by their hand and, first and foremost, for their sake, that is to say, to the benefit of central power. At the same time that the local privileges of the communes are collapsing, toward the time of the reign of Philip the Fair, the Estates General are established.

The priest, still coming from the people, but gradually separated from it by the interest of the group, presides as minister at the king's side, and for five centuries, from Suger to Fleury, he and the legist rule alternately.

If the priest had remained of the people, he would have ruled alone and in his own name; the feudal state would have given way to sacerdotal demagogy. If the freedom of the towns had prevailed, if the communes had persisted, France, carpeted with republics, would never have become a nation. She would have known what Italy experienced: the towns would have absorbed the countrysides, deserted by their inhabitants.

Thanks to the slow extinction of feudalism, France remained strong in her countrysides, like Germany; strong in her towns, like Italy; alive and fecund like the tribe; harmonious and at one like the city. A central power, marvelously potent, was formed there by the alliance of the abstract law of king and priest against the concrete, local law of the barons. The name of the priest and of the king, the representatives of what was most general, that is to say, what was divine in the idea of nation, gave the obscure law of the people a mystical caul, as it were, in which it grew and became stronger. And one fine day, finding itself big and strong, it threw off the swaddlings of infancy. The divine right of king and priest existed only on condition that it express the divine thought, that is to say, the general idea of the people.

In the sacerdotal and monarchic form that it had borne for so long, one could see that the people, whom king and priest had organized against the nobles, nonetheless preserved an instinct independent of one and the other. As adversary to the head of feudalism, that is, to the Emperor, France elevates and stands by the pontiff of Rome, until she can take him off to Avignon and confiscate the pontificate. There was a saying in Provence in the twelfth century: *I would rather be a priest than do such and such*. The same spirit of freedom in politics is present in the forms that absolute monarchy takes. The historical ideal and the habitual boast of the nation was to be the *realm of the Franks*. Early on, the king of France is presented as a citizen king; one need only read Commines and Machiavelli. His parliaments resist him; he himself orders that one *disobey him on pain of disobedience*. An admirable contradiction! The monarchy here is the national arm against the aristocracy, the short route to leveling. As long as the aristocracy remains powerful, every attempt upon the monarchy will fail—however much Marcel may stir up the communes and the Jacquerie raise the countrysides. Privileged liberties must perish under centralizing power, which must reduce everything to dust to make everything equal.

This long leveling of France by monarchical action is what separates our homeland so profoundly from England, with which it does not cease to be compared. England explains France, but by opposition.

Human pride made flesh in a people—this is England. I have already noted the enthusiasm that the man of the North inspires in himself, above all in the unbridled life of coursing and adventure led by the ancient Scandinavians. What will this not amount to when these barbarians betake themselves to that mighty isle, where they will batten on the fat of the land and the gifts of ocean? Rulers of the sea, of a world without law and without limit, bringing together the savage toughness of the Danish pirate, the feudal arrogance of the lordly son of the Normans... How many Tyres must one heap upon Carthages to reach the height of insolence of titanic England?

As penance, this world of arrogance labors under its own contradictions. Composed of two antagonistic principles, industry and feudalism, the egoism of isolation and the egoism of assimilation, it agrees on one point: the acquisition and enjoyment of riches. It has been given gold like sand. Let it satisfy its thirst, let it get drunk if it can. But no, it wants to enjoy and know that it enjoys; it pulls back into the narrow prudence of the *comfortable*. But there in the midst of the material world it holds and relishes, disgust sets in soon enough. Then all is lost: the universe had been reduced to man, man in the enjoyment of real things, and reality is what he lacks. Now it is not tears, not effeminate cries, that are raised, but blasphemies, ragings against heaven. Liberty without God, impious heroism, in literature the *Satanic school*, announced as long ago as Greece, in Aischylos's *Prometheus*, renewed in Hamlet's bitter doubts, finds its ideal form in Milton's Satan. It cries, with him: *Evil, be thou my good!* But it falls back, with Byron, into despair: *Bottomless perdition* [in English in the text—tr.].

England's unbending arrogance has erected an eternal obstacle to the fusion of the races and to the convergence of social stations. Excessively concentrated in a narrow space, they have not mixed the more for all that. And I am not talking about the fatal *remora* that is Ireland, which England can neither drag with her nor cast into the sea. Rather, on his very own island, the Gaul, in Wales, sings of the fast approaching humiliation of England with the return of Arthur and of Bonaparte. Was it so long ago that the Highlanders fought the English at Culloden? Scotland follows but does not love the mistress of the seas; she follows because it is worth her while. Finally, even within England—*old England* [in English in the text—tr.]—are the robust son of the Saxon and the slender son of the Norman not still today distinct? If you do not find the former roaming the woods with Robin Hood, bow in hand, you will find him breaking the machines at Manchester or cut down by the *Yeomanry* [in English in the text—tr.].

Undeniably, English heroism was to usher in modern liberty. In every land it is initially by the hand of the aristocracy, by heroism, by the exaltation of the human sense of self that man liberates himself from authority. The iconoclastic warrior aristocracies of Persia and of Rome look like a veritable Protestantism after India and Etruria. Thus there comes into this world what the priest calls the spirit of evil, Satan, Ahriman, the critical, negative principle, *the one who always says, No*. Once the warrior aristocracy, in the pride of its force, has begun the revolt of humankind, that work is carried forward by the pride of individual reason, by the spirit of dialectic. That spirit spreads quickly from the aristocracy down to the masses; it is the common property of all. But nowhere does it take on more power than in the countries already leveled by the priest and the monarchy.

Thus was revealed at the outer limit of the West a mystery still unknown to the world: heroism is not yet liberty. The heroic people of Europe is England, the free people is France. In England we see the triumph of the old barbarian heroism, the aristocracy, liberty by privilege, all dominated by the Germanic, feudal element. Liberty without equality, unjust, impious liberty is nothing other than unsociableness in society itself. France wants liberty in equality,[1] which is precisely the social genius. The liberty of France is just and sacred. It deserves to be the beginning of the liberty of the world and to bring all peoples together for the first time in a true unity of intelligence and will.

Equality in liberty, the ideal that we are to approach ever more closely without ever reaching it, was to be attained most nearly by the most mixed of peoples, by one in which the opposed fatalities of race and climate are best neutralized one by the other; a people made for action but not for conquest, a people that desires equality for itself and for humankind. This people had to have at the same time a genius for breaking up and for centralizing. The substitution of departments for provinces will explain what I mean. The French Revolution, seemingly materialist in dividing the country into departments named after rivers, nonetheless thereby erased

---

1   Is it necessary to specify that we are speaking of equality of rights, or rather equality of the means of acquiring understanding and the capacity, which should accompany understanding, of exercising political rights?

the nationalities of the provinces, which until then had perpetuated local fatalities in the name of liberty.

That apparently contradictory genius for breaking up and for centralizing must have reproduced itself in our language, making it eminently suited to analyzing and summing up ideas. This double capacity is the Aristotelian genius, which reduces fatal natural aggregates to dust and recovers from this dust artificial aggregates that form little by little the patrimony of human reason—a rightful patrimony that liberty has earned by the sweat of its brow.

Nonetheless, let us admit it: the people, the century when the aristocracy and the priesthood fall at the same time, when the old order of fatality bogs down and falls apart in a swirl of dust—that people and that moment are certainly no thing of beauty. The most mixed of peoples, at a moment when everything is becoming mixed, is not made to please at first glance.

France is not a race, like Germany; it is a nation. Its origin is mixture; action is its life. Wholly caught up by the present, by the real, its character is commonplace, prosaic. The individual derives his glory from his voluntary participation in the whole; he,too, can say: *My name is legion*. Are you going to look for the overbearing personality of the Englishman here, or the calm, the purity, the chaste reserve of Germany? You might as well demand the greensward of May of a dusty road where the crowd has been passing all day long.

Mixture, action, knowing how to get things done: these things, it must be said, hardly rhyme with the idea of innocence and individual dignity. This free, rational genius whose mission is struggle appears in the unappealing forms of war, industry, criticism and dialectics. A mocking smile, the most terrible of negations, does not make for a pretty mouth. We are much in need of physiognomy if we are not to be an ugly people. What could be more grimacing than our first look at the medieval world? Rabelais's Gargantua makes one shudder beside the noble irony of Cervantes and the graceful banter of Ariosto.

For all that, I am not sure that any people involved in life, engaged in action as much as France would have kept its purity better. Consider, on the contrary, how the unmixed races eagerly drink up corruption. Machiavellism, more rare in Germany, often reaches an excess there from which our good sense at least preserves us. It is our special privilege to enter into vice without ruining ourselves, without our senses becoming depraved, without our courage flagging, without becoming entirely degraded. For what pleases us most in the pleasure of evil is taking action, abusing liberty to prove to ourselves that we are free. Thus nothing is lost; our good sense brings us back to the idea of order.

Our particular virtue is not innocence, is not ignorance of evil, childhood's state of grace, virtue without morality; it is experience, it is knowledge, the earnest mother of liberty. Good derived thus from experience is strong and durable; it comes not from blind sympathy, but from the idea of order. It emerges from uncertain, shifting sensibility to enter the domain of immutable reason.

Much will be forgiven this people on account of its noble social instinct. It concerns itself with the liberty of the world; it worries about the most distant misfortune. All humanity vibrates in this people. This lively sympathy is its glory and its beauty. Do not consider the individual separately; contemplate him among the mass of men and above all in action. At a ball or in battle, no one is more galvanized by the feeling of community, which determines the true character of a man. Noble deeds, sublime expressions come to him naturally; he utters words he did not know before. The divine genius of society loosens his tongue. Above all, in a moment of danger, when festivities are lit by a July sun, when fire is met by fire, when lead shot and death spray and ricochet, then stupidity becomes eloquent, cowardice becomes brave; that living dust detaches itself, sparkles, and becomes marvelously beautiful. A fiery poetry goes out from the mass and rolls, with the knell of the tocsin and the echo of the fusillades, from the Pantheon to the Louvre, from the Louvre to the Pont de la Grève. De la Grève? No. To the Pont d'Arcole. And may this word be heard in Italy!

It is the great singularity of the July Revolution to be the original model of a revolution without heroes, without proper names; no individual in whom the glory might have lodged. Society did it all. The revolution of the fourteenth century expiated and epitomized itself in the Maid of Orleans, a pure and touching victim who represented the people and died for it. But here, not one proper name: no one prepared, no one led, no one eclipsed the others. After the victory, one went in search of the hero—and found an entire people.

That marvelous unity had never before been seen on earth. Fifty thousand men had agreed to die for an idea. These were but the braves; countless others fought in spirit; the sudden raising of the tricolore all over France expressed the unanimity of many millions. There was no disorder in this impetuous exultation. They reached agreement without deliberation. The idea of order rose above the action and the tumult. In the momentary absence of a government, of a visible leader, the invisible sovereign of the world appeared: law and justice. In the midst of such confusion, not one murder; not one theft was committed in the course of those three days. In another age, one would have seen in this a miracle; today we simply see the work of human liberty. But what is more divine than order in liberty?

This unique moment, returning to me again and again in memory, keeps up my hope and gives me faith in the moral and religious destiny of my country. Amid the universal unrest that surrounds us, I believe in a peaceful future. For in the end, this people became one for a day in a single common thought; its eyes have seen the glory of the divine idea of order. We have not glimpsed this flash of heavenly light in vain.

Let us have hope and confidence, whatever agitation still fills the beautiful and terrible epoch in which our lives have fallen. It is the peripeteia of a tragedy where the victim is an entire world. An epoch of destruction, of dissolution, of decomposition, of analysis and critique. In philosophy it is by logical analysis, in the social order by that other analysis, by war and revolution, that man passes from one system to another, that he casts off one form to take on another which always gives more to the spirit. But not without cruel effort, not without a painful wrench can he tear himself loose from the fatality at whose breast he has hung so long suspended; the separation still bleeds in the grown man's heart. But it must be: the child must quit its mother, it must walk by itself, it must move forward. Forward, then, child of providence; forward; do not stop. It is God's will! It is God's will! was the cry of the crusades.

This last step away from natural, fatal order, away from the God of the East, is a step toward the social God who is to reveal himself little by little in our very liberty. But if there is a moment when the former effaces himself and disappears and the other is slow to appear, a moment when men believe they see, like Werner, Christ weeping on the altar and himself admitting that there is no God, into what agony of despair will our orphaned world not fall? Ask the unhappy Byron.

How shall we mount from the depths of this abyss toward God?

Humanity, as we have said, moves eternally from decomposition to composition, from analysis to synthesis. In analysis, all relations vanish, all bonds are broken, social and divine unity becomes imperceptible. But gradually relations reappear in knowledge and in society, unity returns to the city and to nature. This world, once reduced to dust, reconstitutes itself and blossoms again in a new creation in which man recognizes, now more beautiful and more pure, the image of the divine order. Knowledge today is in the analytic phase, at the point of minute observation of detail; only thus can its great task begin. Society is reaching the end of an ugly, dirty work of demolition: it is clearing the ground of the debris of a world of fatality that has crumbled. We find the labor long, no doubt. We have been at it for nearly forty years, more than the life of a man, alas. But this is little in the life of a nation. Let us therefore comfort ourselves and take courage; order will return sooner or later, at the least, over our graves.

When unity, and this time unity freely chosen, has reappeared in the social world, and knowledge, by observation of detail, has acquired a legitimate foundation on which to erect its majestic, harmonious edifice, humanity will recognize the accord of a double world, natural and civil, in the benevolent intelligence that has connected the two. But it is primarily by its social sense that humanity will return to the idea of universal order. Once this order has been felt in the limited society of one's own country, the same idea will spread to human society, to the republic of the world.

The Athenian said: Hail, city of Cecrops! And you, will you not say: Hail, city of Providence!

Christianity constructed the moral man. In the concept of equality before God it set up a principle that was later to find fruitful application in the secular world. However, the circumstances that attended its earliest emergence made it less favorable to shared action, to social life than to inactive, solitary contemplation. At its emergence, God was still held captive in materialism and pagan sensuality; man was imprisoned within the narrow confines of the ancient city. Christianity delivered man by breaking the city, freed God by breaking the idols. At this unique moment, man first caught sight of his heavenly home, languished in incurable love for it, folded his arms and, raising his eyes to heaven, awaited the moment of his ascension. *How long, O Lord, how long?* Impatient, idle laborer, you who sit down and claim your wage before the evening, you ask for heaven, but what have you made of the earth that the Lord has given you? To subdue matter, is it enough to break idols, to fast and flee into the desert? You must fight and not flee, and look enemy nature in the eye, know her, use your arts to subjugate her, use her to despise her. You broke up the city of antiquity, a narrow, grudging city that rejected humanity and, emerging from the ruins of that Babel, you spread out over the world. There you are now, divided into kingdoms, into monarchies, speaking twenty different tongues. What about the universal and divine city of which Christian charity gave you a presentiment and which you promised to realize here on earth?

If a social sense is to lead us back to religion, then the organ of that new revelation, the interpreter between God and man, should be the most social of all peoples. The moral world received its Word in Christianity, the child of Judea and of Greece; France will explain the Word of the social world that we now see beginning.

It is at the points of contact between the races, in the collision of their opposed fatalities, in the sudden explosion of intelligence and of liberty that the celestial spark leaps from humanity, the spark that one calls logos, the Word, revelation. Thus when Judea had caught sight of Egypt, Chaldea, and Phoenicia, at the point of the most perfect mixing of the eastern races, the lightning flashed over Sinai and left behind pure, holy unity. When Jewish unity had been fertilized by the genius of Persia and of Greek Egypt, that unity blossomed, opened to embrace all the world in the equality of divine charity. Greece μυθοτόκος, mother of myth and of the word, explicated the Good News; it required nothing less than the marvelous analytic power of the language of Aristotle to pronounce to the nations the logos of the mute East.

At the point of the most perfect mix of the European races, the social word rings out in the form of equality in liberty. Its revelation is successive; its beauty is of no one time or place. This word was not able to produce the ravishing harmony in which the moral word rang out at its birth: the relation between God and man was simple then. The relation of humanity to itself in a divine society, that translation of heaven to earth, is a complex problem whose long solution may last the lifetime of the world; its beauty is in its unfolding, its infinite unfolding.

It belongs to France both to make that new revelation burst upon the world and to explicate it. Every solution, social or intellectual, remains unproductive for Europe until France has interpreted it, translated it, made it available to the people. The reform of the Saxon Luther, which returned the North to its natural opposition against Rome, was democratized by the genius of Calvin. The Catholic reaction of the century of Louis XIV was proclaimed to the world in the exalted dogmatism of Bossuet. The sensism of Locke became European only by way of Voltaire, and of Montesquieu who subjected the development of society to the influence of climate. Moral liberty staked its claim in the name of sentiment in Rousseau, of idea in Kant; but only the influence of the Frenchman reached all Europe.

Thus every solitary thought of the nations is revealed by France. She speaks the Word of Europe as Greece spoke the Word of Asia. What makes her deserving of this mission? It is that the feeling of social generality, both in theory and in practice, develops more quickly in her than in any other people.

As that feeling comes to dawn among other peoples, they become sympathetic toward the French genius, they become France; they confer on her, by their silent imitation at least, the pontificate of the new civilization. What is most young, most fecund in the world is not America, a serious child who will copy others for a long time yet; it is age-old France, made new by the spirit. While civilization locks up the barbarian world in the invincible claws of England and of Russia, France will stir Europe to its depths. Her closest union will no doubt be with the peoples of Latin languages, with Italy and Spain, those two islands that can reach an understanding with the modern world only through the intermediary of France. Then our southern provinces will regain the importance they have lost.

Spain will resist for a long time. The deep monachal demagogy that governs her closes her to the moderate democracy of France. Her monks come from the populace, which they feed. If however this people, reassured on its French side, regains its spirit of adventure, then through it western civilization will reach Africa, already so well leveled by the religion of Mohammed.

Italy, Celtic by race in the provinces of her North, prepared for democracy by the anti-feudal genius of the Church and of the Guelph faction, belongs in her heart to France, which asks no more of her just now. These two countries are sisters; the same practical genius; Salerno and Montpellier, Bourges and Bologna: did they not have a common spirit? Political economy, born in France, resounded in Italy. There is a double echo in the Alps. The fraternity of the two countries will strengthen the social sense of Italy and will make up for what she will always lack in material and political unity. France, head of this great family, will restore to the Latin genius something of the material preponderance that it enjoyed in antiquity, of the spiritual supremacy that it attained in the Middle Ages. In recent times the family treaty that united France, Italy, and Spain in a fraternal alliance has been an empty image of the future union that must bring them together in a community of will and idea. The true embodiment of the future union of Italy and France is Bonaparte. In like fashion Charlemagne was the material figure of the spiritual unity of the feudal and pontifical world that was in the making. Great revolutions are preceded by their prophetic symbols.

Whoever wishes to know the destiny of humankind should plumb the genius of Italy and of France. Rome was the crux of the immense drama whose peripeteia France directs. By placing ourselves on the summit of the Capitoline, we shall embrace with the double regard of Janus both the ancient world that ends here and the modern world, which our native land will lead henceforth down the mysterious road of the future.

Notes and Clarifications

Introduction... and not summary outline. An outline must present all the major points of its subject. An introduction promises only a method, a thread to guide the reader who wishes to study the subject. It is at liberty to make no mention of many things that would have to find a place in even a simple outline.

PAGE 25. **Spirit against matter... this endless struggle.** I heartily congratulate the new apostles who bring us the good news that peace is imminent. But I fear that a treaty will lead to nothing more than to making the spirit material. The industrial pantheism that thinks it is the beginning of a new religion overlooks two things: first, that a religion in any way viable is always the result of a burst of moral liberty, if it is not to end in pantheism, which is the graveyard of religion, and, second, that the last people on earth among whom the human personality will consent to vanish into pantheism is France. Pantheism is in its element in Germany, but here...

PAGE 25. **Of liberty against fatality.** I use "fatality" in its popular sense and mean by this term everything that impedes liberty. How can these two coexist? That question should be put to philosophy, which perhaps would then admit its incapacity on this point more forthrightly.

PAGE 25. **Infiltrating philosophy and history.** This reproach cannot be addressed to M. Guizot. He has respected moral liberty more than any other historian of our time; he has not enslaved history to the fatalism of race or to the fatalism of ideas. So capacious an intellect automatically rejects any exclusive solution. We may confidently expect that the major work M. Villemain is preparing (*Vie de Grégoire VII*) will be no less removed from any teaching that tends to petrify history. A great writer is incapable of misrepresenting and distorting life to make it fit, willy-nilly, into formulas.

PAGE 26. According to M. Ampère, these **magnetic currents** explain the temperature of the surface of the earth better than any other hypothesis; they generally run from east to west.

PAGE 26. **Powerful aromatics.** See Chardin[i] (vol. IV, p. 43, ed. Langlès, 1811), for the prodigal use of perfume in India. At the wedding of a princess of Golconde in 1679, two or three bottles were poured on each guest.

PAGE 26. **Multiplied in excess.** Laknot, ancient capital of Bengal, counted 1,200,000 families in 1538, according to Ayeen-Akbery.[ii]

PAGE 26. **A herd of wild elephants storms…** See the play *Sakontala*.[iii]

PAGE 26. **A thousand bubbling springs.** A vizir of Korasan in Bactriana discovered in the registers of the province that there had once been 42,000 kerises or underground canals. **Fecund and homicidal heat.** "In a morning dream I saw the angel of death fleeing barefoot and at top speed away from the city of Raga. I said to him: 'And even you take flight!'" For this citation of a Persian poet, and for all the details that follow here, see Chardin, vol. II, p. 413; vol. III, p. 405; vol. IV, pp. 57, 58, 125, 127. See also the magnificent work by Porter (*Ker Porter's Travels*, 2 vols., 1818), which alone is authoritative with respect to art.

PAGE 27. **By killing himself before the very eyes …** *Asiatic Researches*, III, 344; V, 268.

PAGE 27. **Within fatality.** J. Goerres, introduction to *Das Heldenbuch von Iran aus dem Shah Nameh des Firdussi*, 1820.

PAGE 27. **The gift of the Nile.** Ὅτι Αἴγυπτος…ἐστὶ Αἰγυπτίοισι ἐπίκτητός τε γῆ καὶ δῶρον τοῦ ποταμοῦ. Herod, II, 5.

PAGE 27. **The great Albuquerque…** *Commentarios do grando Alfonso de Alboquerque, capitan general dà India,* etc., 1576, by the son of Albuquerque. See also *L'Asia Portugueza*, by Barros and his continuators.

PAGE 28. **Who fights with his two hands… does not hesitate to eat the loaves of proposition**. Judges 3, 15; 1 Kings 21.

PAGE 30. **Interceding with the father of the gods in behalf of man…**

> Ζεῦ πάτερ, ἠδ' ἄλλοι μάκαρες θεοί αἰὲν ἐόντες,
> Μήτις ἔτι πρόφρων ἀγανός καὶ ἤπιος ἔστω
> Σκηπτοῦχος βασιλεὺς, μηδέ φρεσὶν αἴσιμα εἰδώς·
> Ἀλλ' αἰεὶ χαλεπός τ' εἴη, καὶ αἴσυλα ῥέζοι·
> Ὡς οὔτις μέμνηται Ὀδυσσῆος θείοιο
> Λαῶν, οἷσιν ἄνασσε, πατήρ δ'ὣς ἤπιος ἦεν…
>
> Odyssey

PAGE 31. **Rome, etc.** Development and proof of these matters belongs more properly to my *Histoire Romaine*.

PAGE 32. **The Semitic world resisted...** See the representation of the long struggle between the Semitic world and the Indo-Germanic world in my *Histoire Romaine*, II, ch. 2.

PAGE 33. **Reread the *Phaido* at Utica, died at Philippi reciting Euripides, and cried out in Greek under the blows of Brutus's dagger**. See Plutarch, *Lives* of Cato and Brutus, and Suetonius, *Lives of the Caesars*.

PAGE 33. **Rome rejected the bacchanals.** How the ideas of Greece and of the East invaded Rome is one of the principal subjects of my *Histoire Romaine*, III, ch. 2, "Dissolution de la Cité."

PAGE 33. **Gloomy Serapis, yet another god of life and death.** Hadrian writes: "Those who worship Serapis are Christians and those who call themselves bishops of Christ are devoted to Serapis... They [those of Alexandria] have only one God, to whom Christians, Jews, and all nations pay homage." Saturnin, *Vopiscus*, ch. 8, Letter of Hadrian. See the article by Guignaut following vol. 5 of Burnouf's translation of Tacitus.

PAGE 33. **Below the Capitol... gory Mithras...** The celebrated Mithriatic bas relief of the Villa Borghese, now in the Louvre, was consecrated in the underground passage that led beneath the Capitoline Hill from the Campus Martius to the Forum. **The horrible bull sacrifice...** See the memoir of Lajart and Creuzer's *Symbolique*, notes by Guignaut.[iv]

PAGE 34. **Liberty, famished for pain, rushed to the amphitheater and relished being put to death...** We have, among others, the letter of St. Ignatius, bishop of Antioch, written to the Christians of Rome, who wanted to deliver him and so deprive him of the martyr's crown:

"It is my hope to greet you soon in the irons of Christ, should it be my good fortune to consummate what I have so well begun. What I fear is that your charity might do me wrong. For I shall never find an equal occasion to reach God. If you favor me with your silence, I shall be his... You are not envious; you teach others. I only wish to accomplish your teachings. Let me become the repast of beasts; I am the wheat of God; ground by their teeth, may I yet become the true bread of God... Oh, may I have the pleasure of the beasts that are being prepared for me... I write you yet living, but eager for and longing for death (ὀναίμην τῶν θηρίων τῶν ἐμοὶ ἡτοιμασμένων...ζῶν γὰρ γράφω ὑμῖν, ἐρῶν τοῦ ἀποθάνειν)."

3. Introduction to World History 67

The authenticity of this letter is critically established; it does not belong to the apocryphal letters of this church father. (*SS. Patrum qui temporibus apostolicis floruerunt, Barnabae, Clementis, Herma, Ignatii, Polycarpiopera*. Recensuit J. Clericus, Amstelaedami, 1724, pp. 25-30.)

Page 34. **"I see before me the gladiator lie..."**

> I see before me the gladiator lie.
> He leans upon his hand—his manly brow
> Consents to death! But conquers agony.
> And his droop'd head sinks gradually low—
> And through his side the last drops, ebbing slow
> From the red gash, fall heavy, one by one,
> Like the first of a thunder-shower; and now
> The arena swims around him—he is gone,
> Ere ceased the inhuman shout which hail'd the wretch who won.
>
> He heard it, but he heeded not—his eyes
> Were with his heart, and that was far away.
> He reck'd not of the life he lost nor prize,
> But where his rude hut by the Danube lay.
> There were his young barbarians all at play,
> There was their Dacian mother—he, their sire,
> Butcher'd to make a Roman holiday—
> All this rush'd with his blood—shall he expire,
> And unavenged?—Arise! Ye Goths, and glut your ire!
> . . . .
> While stands the Coliseum, Rome shall stand;
> When falls the Coliseum, Rome shall fall;
> And when Rome falls—the world...

Childe Harold, IV, 191-192 [in English in text—tr.]

Page 35. **From the Bosporos to Batavia.** On the establishment of the Franks on the shores of the Pontos Euxeinos and their return to the land of the Batavi, see *Panegyr. vet*, V, 18 and Zozim., I, p. 66.[v]

Page 35. **Under their savage and pitiless rule domestic slavery...** It is clear that the Franks accorded slaveholders no such special protection as did the Burgundians and the Visigoths. See *Collection des Historiens de France*, IV, *lex Burgundiorum*, tit. XXXIX and *lex Visigothorum*, Lib. III, tit. II, par. 3, 4, 5; tit. III, par. 9. Lib. V, tit. IV, par. 17, 18, 21; tit. VII, par. 2, 3, 10, 11, 13, 14, 16, 17, 21, 21. Lib. VI, tit. III, 6; tit. IV, 1, 9, 11; tit. V, 9, 20. Lib. VII, tit. I, par. 6; tit. II, par. 21; tit III, par. 1, 2, 4. Lib. IX, tit. I.

PAGE 36. **Isn't that Jerusalem?** ... "Videres mirum quiddam; ipsos infantulos, dum obviam habent quaelibet castellam vel urbes, si haec esset Jerusalem ad quam tenderent rogitare." *Guibert*, lib. I.[vi]

PAGE 36. **The countless arches of the cathedrals.** About the year 1000, the medieval world, astonished to have survived the moment long announced for its destruction (*adventate mundi vespero*, etc.) set to work with childlike joy renovating most of its religious edifices. In the words of a contemporary, it was as if the world, bestirring itself and casting off its old rags, had donned the white robe of the churches: "erat enim instar ac si mundus ipse excutiendo semet, rejecta vetustate passim candidam ecclesiarum vestem indueret." Rad. Glaber, III, 4.[vii]

PAGE 36. **The five thousand marble statues that crown the cathedral of Milan.** This astonishing number was assured me by the learned and precise writer to whom we owe the description of that cathedral: Gaetano Franchetti, *Storia e descrizione del Duomo di Milano*, Milan, 1821. In-folio. See also the colossal work of Boisserée on the Cologne cathedral. In a moment of perfect resemblance, the description remains incomplete, as does the monument.

PAGE 36. **A man in black... a legist against the priestly alb.** In the middle of the thirteenth century the influence of men of law suddenly appeared in legislation that had been entirely feudal and ecclesiastic until then. St. Louis and Frederick II publish their codes almost simultaneously, and for the first time Roman law emerges openly opposite feudal law. In the *Établissements* the pandects are cited pedantically—and often poorly understood. To these legists we probably owe the firmness of the pious Louis IX toward the court of Rome. Nonetheless, I confess, I find that this cortege of prosecutors fairly casts a shadow over the poetic picture of the sainted king meting out patriarchal justice to his subjects under the oak tree at Vincennes. Little by little the legists become the masters; in the fourteenth century they reign supreme. It was one of these *knights of law*, Guillaume de Nogaret, who took it upon himself to deliver the challenge of Philip the Fair to Boniface VIII. All Christendom was indignant. Dante exclaims: "I see the man of the fleurs de lis (*lo fiordaliso*) enter Anagni and see Christ captive in his vicar. I see him mocked and insulted anew, given to drink of vinegar and gall, and put to death between thieves." *Purgatorio*, XX, 86. I give the entire passage in Italian below.

GERMANY

However severe the judgment that follows, the reader should not accuse me of bias against dear, learned Germany, to whose works I am so much indebted and where I have such valued friends. No one is more cognizant of the touching goodness and adorable purity of German customs, of the wide learning of her cultivated men, of the vast and profound genius of her philosophers. Under the Restoration the French public became their willing disciple and patiently received what it was seen fit to reveal to it of that mysterious land. In a few years France might perhaps have been as conquered by the ideas of northern Germany as was Italy by the arms of southern Germany. Nonetheless, for all its superior learning, does that land today have sufficient verve and originality to pretend to take the lead over France? The preeminent figure of its literature is eighty years old; all its remaining great men—Schelling and Hegel, Goerres and Creuzer—are mature figures that have borne their best fruit. If we except two young men of promise, Gans and Otfried Müller, Germany presents little more than a great workshop of erudition and criticism, an immense laboratory of editions, recensions, animadversions, etc. This is a people of erudite men of superior training and superior discipline. The future will decide what that superior discipline is worth in matters of war and of letters.

Page 38. **The most hospitable of men.** In the Middle Ages and in the high antiquity of the North, the host sets a condition for the pilgrim, the bard, the messenger, the mendicant (who are often the same): that he respond to an enigmatic question. Odin, in the guise of a pilgrim, also proposes questions to his hosts: he has traveled forty-two times among the peoples, under as many names. "Then came a penniless traveler who wanted to go to the Holy Sepulcher; his name was Tragemund and he knew seventy-two kingdoms" (German lay of the "Tattered Cloak" or "King Orendel"). See the questions of the pilgrim in *Tragemundslied* and the article by J. Grimm on this lay, *Altdeutsche Wälder*, 7, 1813.

The tradition of St. Andrew, mentioned in the Golden Legend, is similar with respect to form. The devil, in the guise of a pretty woman, had insinuated himself upon a bishop and wanted to seduce him. A pilgrim suddenly appears at the door, knocks hard and calls loudly. The bishop asks the woman whether the stranger must be admitted. "Let us pose a difficult question," she replies. "If he knows the answer, he will be admitted. If not, he will be sent away as ignorant and unworthy to appear before the bishop. Let us ask what is the most admirable small thing God has done." The pilgrim answers: "The excellence and the variety of faces." The woman then says: "Let us ask him a more difficult question: At what point is the earth higher than the heavens?" The pilgrim replies: "On the empyrean, where the body of Jesus Christ lies" (*as flesh and thus as earth*). "Fine," says the woman. "Let him be asked a third question, very difficult and very obscure, so that we may know whether he is worthy to be seated at the bishop's table. What is the distance from earth to heaven?" And the pilgrim to the messenger: "Go back to the one who sent you and put that question to him, for he knows more about this than I do: he covered the distance when he was cast into the abyss, and I have never fallen from heaven." The messenger was seized with fear and had hardly brought back the response when the evil one vanished. A similar story appears among the sagas of the north.

PAGE 38. **The communal table is an altar.** The table has a sacred character also among the Celtic peoples, viz. the famous round table of King Arthur. But it is mainly in Germany and the North that a man gives himself over with unthinking abandon to those barbaric feasts where, disarmed by drunkenness, he puts himself at the mercy of his comrades' good faith. These intemperate habits are recognized in the laws of Norway: "The head of household must render judgment in a state of sobriety; if one of them has eaten or drunk too much, there shall be no judgment on that day." *Magnusar Konongs laga-baetirs gula-things-lang sive jus commune Norvegicum*, Havniae, 1817, in-4. This is a reform of ancient law made in 1274 by King Magnus on the Island of Guley. Norway followed this code for five centuries.

PAGE 38. **Baptism by beer... laughable, touching mysteries of old Germany... sacred symbolism... solemn initiations.** This little-known subject deserves to be treated in some detail. I will give particular emphasis to the societies of hunters and artisans.[viii]

Grimm has collected 205 hunting calls (*Alt. Wälder*, III, 3, 4, 5, "Waidsprüche und Jägerschreie"). Moeser claims to have known more than 750. The language of the hunt as it is preserved in these calls and songs is infinitely varied and poetic. Stalkers can tell from the track not only the species but also the sex, age, and fecundity of the animals with amazing precision. They had 72 marks to distinguish the track of a stag; most of those marks had a special name. Even in this superficial sense, the language of German hunters and shepherds is a poetic language, since it has many expressions that are also images. The mountainous countrysides of Tyrol, Switzerland, the Palatinate, and Swabia are the most rich in such expressions.

The questions and answers of journeymen artisans bear a close and incontestable resemblance to those of hunters; here too one finds symbolic colors and numbers (3, 7). By language, by wise, prudent, and precise replies, a host or a companion artisan or hunter recognizes a colleague, knows that he is in the company of a peer whom he can trust. Even robber bands, comparable, by poaching, to hunters, have devised a language full of poetic expressions and cultivated it since time out of mind. The ancient giants,[ix] heroes and dwarves, exchange questions and demand signs. Similarly, journeymen companions and hunters have represented the whole poetic, ludic side of their way of life in regular formulas, instructive and playful by turns, where the deeper, serious sense is concealed by good humor.

Q. Brave hunter, what have you sniffed today? A. A noble stag and a wild boar; what more could I ask for? Q. Brave hunter, tell me: what is the best weather for you? A. Snow and thaw, that's the best weather. Q. Tell me, brave hunter, what should the hunter do when he gets up early in the morning? A. He should ask God to make the day lucky, more lucky than ever; he should take his hound by the leash to find the best tracks; he should live according to God, and he'll never have bad luck. Q. Brave hunter, tell me why a hunter is called a master hunter? A. A skilled hunter with sure aim obtains from the princes and barons the favor of being called master of the seven liberal arts [*der freien Künste*].

Q. Tell me, my good hunter, where did you leave your fair, your excellent little lady? A. I left her beneath a majestic tree, under its green foliage, and I'll go join her there. Long life to the girl all dressed in white who wishes me luck and prosperity every day! Every day, with the dew, I find her at the same spot. When I am hurt, it's the fine girl who heals me. "I wish the hunter health and happiness," she says. "May he find a good stag!"

Q. Tell me, brave hunter, what the wolf says to the stag in winter. A. "Come closer, come closer, you stringy, skinny baby, you're going down my throat. I'll carry you off into the wild wood."

Q. Brave hunter, tell me please, what makes the noble stag leave the field for the forest? A. The light of day and the brightness of dawn. Q. Brave hunter, tell me, what did the noble stag do when he left the wood for the field? A. He trampled the oats and the rye, and the peasants are furious.

Q. Brave hunter's boy, do your duty and I'll give you your hunter's rights. Be quick and canny and you'll be my favorite boy. On your feet, you lazy-bones, you sluggards who prefer to lie abed. And you, wise hunter, lay out the kit, do the work of your father. You, proud hunter, will lead my pack to the wood. And you, young whip, what have you scented? A. Good luck and good health will be our lot. I scent a stag and a boar. He just passed in front of me. It would be better to have taken him.

Q. Brave hunter, not to annoy you, where are they running now? A. They are running on the fields and in the roads. So much the better for the ordinary game. So much the worse for the noble stag. Do you hear my dog's voice? They are chasing in the hills and the glens. They're on the right track. I hear them sound the horn. They are about to kill the noble stag. Yes, may God favor us. May the noble stag be lying on his side. May the horn be telling us that the stag has been taken, and we'll come running with a great shout. God give us all long life.

On your feet, cook and steward. Prepare a fine soup and a barrel of wine today, so that we can all live merrily.

Q. Tell me, gentle hunter, where do you find the first track of the noble stag? A. When the noble stag leaves his mother's side and leaps through the foliage and over the green. Q. Tell me, gentle hunter, what is the highest track? A. When the noble stag polishes his noble antlers, when he rubs the branches, when he has disturbed the foliage with his noble crown.

Q. Tell me kindly and politely, which is the proudest, the highest, the noblest of the animals? A. I shall tell you. The noble stag is the proudest, the squirrel is the highest, and the hare is regarded as the most noble. One knows him by his track. Q. Brave hunter, tell me quickly, what is the hunter's reward? A. I'll tell you right away. The day is fine, and so all the hunters are merry and content; the weather is calm and clear, and so all the hunters are drinking good wine. So I'll stay with them today and forever. Q. Tell me, brave hunter, who would be the least useful attendants for my prince or my lord? A. A well-outfitted hunter who will not laugh, a hound that trots around and takes nothing, a lay-about whippet: these are unuseful attendants. Q. Tell me, brave hunter, what goes ahead of the stag in the wood? A. His smoking breath goes ahead of him in the wood. Q. Tell me what the noble stag did in the clear running water? A. He quenched his thirst, he revived his young heart. Q. Brave hunter, tell me, what makes the noble stag's horn so handsome? A. It's little worms that make the noble stag's horn so handsome. Q. Tell me, brave hunter, what makes the forest white, the wolf white, the sea wide, and where all wisdom comes from. A. I shall tell you. Age makes the wolf white and snow, the forests; water makes the sea wide, and all wisdom comes from fair maidens.

Up, up, lords and ladies [further on: "all you pretty maidens"], we'll go and see a noble stag. On your feet, lords and ladies, counts and barons, knights, pages, and you, too, boon companions who want to go with me into the forest. On your feet, in the name of the one who created the wild beast and the domestic animal. Up, up, rested and well disposed like the noble stag; up, rested and content like the hunters. Up, steward and cook.

See him run, hunters, it's a noble stag, I am certain. He is running, he pauses [*wanks und schwanks*]. The poor thing no longer thinks of his mother. He runs over the roads and the pastures. God save my sweetheart. The noble stag crosses the river and the valley. How I love my girl's rosy mouth. Look, the noble stag makes a turn. I'd like to take my girl by the hand. The noble stag runs across the roads. I would like to lie on my true love's bosom. The noble stag leaps over the heather. May God protect my beloved in the white dress. The noble stag runs over the morning dew. How I love to see my pretty girl.

(The hunters drink after bringing down the stag.) Q. Hunter, tell me, brave hunter, what should the hunter keep from doing? A. From talking and chattering. It's the undoing of the hunter.

Q. Brave hunter, kind hunter, tell me when the noble stag is most well off? A. When the hunters sit and drink beer and wine, then the stag is usually very well off.

When the hunters ask about their hounds. Q. Could you tell me, brave hunter, if you have seen my hounds running or heard them cry? A. Yes, brave hunter. They are on the right track, I assure you. There were three hounds. One was white, white, white and was chasing the stag with all his might. The other was pale, pale, pale and was following the stag over hill and dale. The third was red, red, red and was chasing the noble stag until he was dead.

When the hunter gives the quarry to the hound, he says, Companion, fine companion, you chased the stag well today as he leapt over the fields and the roads. That's why he gave us the hunter's rights. Oh, oh, companion, all honor and thanks. Isn't that a fine start? The hunters can relax and drink the wine of the Rhine and the Neckar. Much thanks, faithful companion, all honor and thanks.

Artisans, far more closely associated than hunters, admitted new members to their corporations only after they had undergone solemn initiations, whose form the reader will find below. Excerpt from the book of Frisius, examiner at Altenberg, about 1700 (*Altdeutsche Wälder, durch die Brüder Grimm*, III, Cassel, 1813):

Reception of a Companion Smith. The apprentice must appear before the companions on the day when they meet at the hostel. The speeches and procedures that take place are of three kinds: 1. fan the fire, 2. restore the fire, 3. instruct.

A chair is placed in the middle of the room. An elder drapes a towel around his neck so that the two ends fall into a basin standing on the table. The one who wants to fan the fire rises and says: "May I be permitted to go fetch what is needed to fan the fire. One, two, three. May I be permitted to remove the companions' basins. Companions, what fault do you find with me?"

Answer: The companions find lots of fault with you: *you limp, you stink.*[1] If you can find someone who *limps and stinks* even more, stand up and hang your filthy rags around his neck.

---

1   Two German words that sound alike and that one always finds together in the old songs to describe what is unpleasant. E.g., in a ranz (Recueil de J.-R. Wyss, Berne, 1826): "Tryh yha, allsamma:/Die hinket, die stinket," etc. [Michelet's footnote; translator's and editor's notes, indicated by Roman numerals, are given as endnotes. —Ed.]

The companion pretends to search, and the one who wants to be received is brought in. As soon as the first man sees him, he hangs the towel around his neck and has him sit down on a chair. The elder then says to the apprentice: "Find three sponsors who will make you a companion." One then restores the fire. The godson says to his sponsor: "Sponsor, how much must I pay for the honor of bearing your name?" A. A basket of prawns, a piece of boiling beef, a cup of wine, a slice of ham, so that we can be merry...

Instruction. My dear godson, I'm going to teach you many customs of the trade, but you may well already know more than I myself have ever learned and forgotten. In any case, I'll tell you when it's good to go traveling. Between Easter and Whitsun, when one's shoes are well sewn and one's purse well furnished, one can set out. Take leave of your master politely one Sunday noon after dinner, never during the week. It's not customary in the trade to leave work in the middle of the week. Say to him: "Master, I thank you for teaching me an honorable trade; may it please God that I make it good to you and yours some day." Say to the mistress: "Mistress, I thank you for taking care of my laundry. If I return some day, I'll pay you for your trouble." Next, go find your friends and associates and say to them: "God protect you; no hard feelings." If you have money, order a quart of beer and treat your friends and associates. When you reach the gates of the town, take three feathers in your hand and blow them away. One will fly over the walls, the other onto the water, and a third straight in front of you. Which one will you follow?

If you followed the first over the walls, you might well fall and you would be done out of your life, your mother would be out a son, and we would be out a godson: that would make three misfortunes. If you followed the second onto the water, you could drown, etc. No, don't be foolish. Follow the one that flies straight ahead, and you'll come to a pond where you'll see a group of men all dressed in green and seated on the shore, who'll shout: "Woe! Woe!"

Keep going. You'll hear a mill that says endlessly: "Go back, go back!" Keep going until you reach the mill. If you're hungry, go in and say: "Hello, good mother. Does the calf still have fodder? How is your dog? Is the cat strong and healthy? Do the hens lay well? How are the girls? Do they have many admirers? If they're still honest, all the men will seek them out." "Ah," the good mother will say, "it's a fine boy with good manners. He cares about my animals and my girls." She'll go to get a ladder to fetch you down a sausage from the flue. Don't let her go up the ladder; go up yourself and bring down the sausage pole for her. Don't be so rude as to take the longest one and stuff it in your sack; wait for her to give it to you. When you have it, thank her and go on your way. There may be a miller's axe there that you stare at, thinking you'd like to make such a tool yourself, but the miller would think you want to steal it. Don't look at it any longer, for millers are unfriendly people. They have long ear picks. If they should swat you on the ears with one, you'd be out of a life, your mother, etc.

You'll go on and find yourself in a deep forest where the birds sing, great and small, and you'll want to be as merry as they are. Then you'll see a fine merchant coming, dressed in red velvet and on horseback, who'll say to you: "Good luck, comrade! Why so merry?"

"Well," you'll say, "why should I not be merry, since I'm carrying my father's whole worth?" He'll think that you have some two thousand talers in your pocket and suggest a trade. Don't do it, neither the first time nor the second. If he asks a third time, make a trade with him, but watch out, *don't give him your coat first.* Let him give you his. Because if you gave him yours first, he could go off at a gallop. He has four feet, you have only two and you'd never catch up with him. After the trade, go on your way and don't look back. If he should see you looking back, he might think that you have cheated him. He could double back and come after you and put your life in danger. Go your way.

Farther on you'll find a spring. Have a drink and don't muddy the water. Another companion might come and want a drink. Farther on you'll see a gibbet. Will you be sad or happy? My godson, you should be neither sad nor happy, nor should you be afraid that you'll be hanged, but you should be pleased that you've arrived in a town or a village. If it's a town and they ask you at the gates where you're coming from, don't say that you've come a long way. Say, *"From not far,"* and name the closest village. In many places the watchmen won't let anyone enter. One leaves one's bundle at the gate and goes to get the token. Go to the hostel[2] to request the token from the father of the companions. Say as you go in: "Hello, good luck, God save our honorable trade. Master and companions, let me see the father."

If the father is at home, say to him: "Father, I'd like to ask you to give me the token of the companions so that I can pick up my bundle at the town gate." The father will give you a horseshoe or a large ring as a token, and you can fetch your bundle. On your way, you'll see a little white dog with a fine curly tail. "Oh," you'll say, "I'd like to catch that little dog and cut off his tail to make me a fine plume." Don't do it, godson. You could lose your token if you throw it at him or you could kill him, and you would lose an honorable trade. When you've returned to the father at the hostel, say to him: "I wanted to ask you, by the honor of the trade, to give me lodging, me and my bundle." The father will say to you: "Set down your bundle. But be careful and don't hang it on the wall the way the peasants hang their

---

2 Each trade had its hostel at the home of a senior companion.

baskets. Put it right under the workbench. If the father doesn't lose his hammers, you'll not lose your bundle either."

In the evening, when they're going to table, stay in your place near the door. If the companion father says to you: "Smith, come and eat with us," don't accept right away. If he asks you a second time, go to table and eat. If you cut the bread, first cut a small slice without haste so that you'll hardly be noticed, and in the end, cut a nice big slice and eat your fill, like the others.

When the father drinks your health, you can drink, too. If there is a lot to drink, drink a lot; if little, drink little. But if you have a lot of money, drink up and ask if there's an errand boy, say you'd like to stand them a pitcher of beer. When night comes, ask if the father has need of a smith who sleeps well. He'll reply: "I sleep well myself. I don't need a smith for that." The next day, when you've gotten up early, the father will say to you: "Smith, what was all that noise about [at morning]?" Answer: "I don't know a thing. The cats are fighting and I don't dare stay in bed."

The elder will then say: "The one whose name does not appear in our letters, in the registers of the society, let him stand up and appear before the table of the masters and companions. Let him pay a groschen as scribe's fee, a good tip for the secretary, and we'll enroll him, like me and every other good companion, because these are the practices and customs of the trade, and the practices and customs of the trade should be preserved, whether here or elsewhere. No one is to talk about the customs and the stories of the trade, about anything the masters and companions, young and old, may have done at the hostel."

Reception of a Companion Cooper. One first asks permission to admit before the assembled coopers the young man to be received as a companion, whom one calls Goatskin Apron. When he has been admitted, the companion who is to "plane" him speaks thus:

Good fortune to you all. May God honor this honorable company, masters and companions both. I do declare, by your leave, someone—I don't know who—is following me around with a goatskin: a hoop-murderer, a stave-wrecker, a knockabout, a traitor to our company. He comes to the threshold, pulls back, says he's not to blame, comes in with me. He says that when he's been "planed," he'll be as good a companion as any. So I do declare, gracious and valued masters and companions, Goatskin here present has come looking for me and has asked me please to "plane" him according to the customs of the trade, to accord his name honor, since it's the practice of our company. I certainly thought that he would find a number of companions, with seniority, who have forgotten more of the customs of the trade than I, a youngster here, have ever learned, but then I didn't want to refuse. I've consented because it would have been ridiculous to refuse and would have got him off on the wrong foot for his travels. So I'm going to "plane" him and instruct him the way my sponsor instructed me, and what I can't teach him he can learn on his travels. But I beg you, masters and companions, if I get a few things wrong in the process, or many, not to hold it against me, but to correct me instead and teach me better.

With your permission, I shall ask three questions. First, I'll ask if there is a master or companion who knows something against me, or against Goatskin here present, or against his master. Let him stand up and make his declaration. If he knows something against me, I'll submit to the discipline of this honorable company, as is the custom; if he knows something against Goatskin here present, then he will not be considered worthy of being received as a companion either by me or by all the honorable company; but if it's against his master, the master will accept punishment, too, as is the custom. With your permission, I'll climb up on the table.

At this point the apprentice enters the room with his sponsor. He is carrying a stool on his shoulders and climbs, with the stool, on to the table. The other companions come up one after the other and pull him three times by the stool to make him fall on to the tabletop, but his sponsor comes to his rescue and holds him by the hair to keep him upright. This is what is called "planing." Then he is repeatedly baptized in beer.

The sponsor says: You can all see: the head I'm holding onto is as empty as a whistle. It has a pink mouth, for a certainty, that eats up many a morsel and knocks back many a slug. It's trade custom here as elsewhere that the one being "planed" has, besides his sponsor, two other companion "planers." Look at all the companions and choose two as your mates. What name will you take as your "plane" name? Choose a nice one, a short one, and one the girls will like. All the world likes a short name. They'll drink your health with wine or beer. And now pay the same baptismal fee as everybody else, and the masters and companions will be pleased with you.

By your leave, Master X, I ask if you vouch that your apprentice knows his trade. Has he trimmed and cut the staves well and the hoops? Did he go for beer and wine often and chasing after girls? Was he good at cards and contests? Did he sleep long, work little, eat much, and stretch out his Sundays and holidays? Did he complete his years of apprenticeship like a good apprentice? A. Yes. Q. Did you learn everything? A. Yes. Q. Oh, that's not possible. Look at the masters and companions around you. There are good ones and old ones, but not a one of them knows everything, and you claim you do? You're wide of the mark. Do you think you can become a master? A. Yes. Q. You'll have to be a companion first. Do you want to go traveling? A. Yes.

Q. On your way you'll see a dung heap and black crows on top of it, who'll cry: "He's leaving! He's leaving!" What to do? Ought you to turn back or go ahead? Answer yes or no... You should keep going and say to yourself: Black crows, you'll not be my prophets. Farther on, before a village, three old women will look at you and say: "Ah, young companion, turn back, because in another quarter-mile you'll come to a great forest where you'll get lost and no one will know where you are." Are you going to turn back? A. Yes. Q. Oh, no, don't do it. It would be ridiculous for you to listen to the tales of three old women. At the end of the village, you'll pass in front of a mill that says: "Go back! Go back!" What will you do? Three sorts of advisors: first the crows, then the three old women, and now the mill. Something bad is going to happen to you. Turn back or go on? A. Yes. Q. Keep to your way and say: "Mill, you go your way and I'll go mine." Farther on, you'll come to the big, boundless forest that the three old women told you about, deep and dark. You'll be white with fear as you cross it, but there is no other way. The birds will sing, great and small; a sharp cold wind will blow; the trees will bend, see and saw, clink and clank: they'll crack and groan as if they were about to come crashing down and you will be in great danger. "Ah," you'll say, "if only I'd stayed home with mother." Because in the end a tree could fall on you and crush you and you'd be out your young life, your mother would be out her son, and I'd be out my godson. Are you going to turn around? Or do you want to go on? You must.

When you leave the forest you will find yourself in a fine meadow where you will see a fine pear tree standing covered with fine yellow pears, but the tree will be quite tall. Stand under it for a while and open your mouth. If a fresh breeze comes, the pears will fall into your mouth aplenty. Is this what one should do? (The apprentice answers Yes and one "planes" him and pulls his hair, as is proper.) Don't try to climb the tree. The peasant could come and give you a beating. Peasants are crude people who will hit you two or three times on the same place. Pay attention: I'm going to give you a piece of advice. You are a strong young companion. Take the tree by the trunk and shake hard. The pears will fall, lots of them. Are you going to gather them all? A. Yes. Q. Oh, no. You should leave some and say to yourself: "Who knows? Perhaps another fine companion will come through the forest up to this pear tree. He'll want to eat some pears, but he won't be strong enough to shake the tree. It would be doing him a favor to leave some for him."

As you go on, you'll come to a stream crossed by a very narrow bridge, and on the bridge you'll meet a girl with a goat. But the bridge is so narrow that you can't pass. What will you do? Well, push the girl and the goat into the water so that you have no trouble crossing. What do you say to that? A. Yes. Q. Oh, no. I'm going to give you different advice. Take the goat on your shoulders and the girl in your arms and cross with your bundle, and you'll arrive all three on the other side. You can take the girl for your wife, since you need a wife, and slaughter the goat. Its meat is good for the wedding feast, and its skin will make you a fine apron or a satchel for your wife... (The apprentice is "planed" again.)

Farther on you'll see the town. When you're close, stop a bit and put on shoes and clean stockings. Ask for the hostel kept by a master, go straight there, greet everyone and say: "Father of the companions, I would like to ask you to put me up, by the honor of the trade—me and my bundle, and to permit me to sit down on your bench and put my bundle underneath. Please don't make me sit before the door. I'll behave in keeping with the customs of the trade, as is becoming to a polite companion."

The father will say to you: "If you will be a good son, go inside and set down your bundle, for the love of God." If you see the mother when you go inside, say to her: "Hello, good mother." If the father has daughters, call them "sister" and call the companions "brother." In many places they have a fine room with stags' antlers mounted on the wall. Hang your bundle on one of those antlers; if it has rained and you're wet, hang your coat near the stove, and your shoes and stockings, too, and dry them out so that they'll be fresh and ready when you leave next day. Is that what you'll do? A. Yes. Q. Oh, no. If the father is good enough to give you lodging, go inside, put your bundle underneath the bench by the door, sit down on the bench, and keep still.

At evening the father will have you shown to bed, but if the sister wants to light your way up ... so that you're not afraid , , , watch out. When you get upstairs and find your bed, thank her, wish her good night and tell her that she should go back downstairs, for the love of God, that you'll soon be in bed.

Next morning, when it's light and the others get up, you can stay in bed until the sun strikes you. No one will come to wake you, and you can sleep as long as you please. What do you say to that? A. Yes. Q. Oh, no. When you see it's time to get up, get out of bed, and when you come downstairs, say good morning to the father, the mother, the brothers and the sisters. They may ask you how you slept. Tell them your dream to make them laugh.

If you want work in town ... sometimes the elder should look for a job for you, sometimes the brother, and sometimes you yourself, according to different local custom. Go find the elder and say: "Companion, I would like to ask you, according to the practice and custom of the trade, to please find me a job; I want to work here." The elder will reply: "Companion, I'll take care of it." ... And at this point you will go out for a beer or to see the fine houses in town. Won't you? A. Yes. Q. Oh, no. You should go back to the hostel until the elder returns, because it's better for you to wait for him than to make him wait for you. But meanwhile you'll meet three masters on your way. The first has lots of staves and hoops; the second has three pretty daughters and offers beer and wine; the third is poor. Which one will you go to work for? If you work for the first, you'll become a strong cooper; with the second, who offers beer and wine and has pretty daughters, you'll be happy, as they say; there one makes fine presents, one drinks well, and one hops about with pretty girls. And with the poor master?... I understand: you want to make your fortune. Which one will you work for? Don't disdain anyone. You must work for the poor one as for the rich one... The elder will tell you when he returns: "Companion, I looked for a job and I found one." Reply: "Just a minute, companion. I'll send for a pitcher of beer." But if you don't have money, say to him: "Companion, I'm momentarily low on funds, but if we see each other again today or tomorrow, I'll show you my appreciation."

The master will give you your task and your tools. When you have been at work for a while, your tools will stop cutting. "Master," you'll say, "I don't know whether it's because the tools won't cut or because I've lost my taste for work. Turn the grindstone so that I can sharpen my tools." Is that what you'll do? A. Yes. Q. Oh, no. If you begin work and there are a number of other companions, you can't feel stung when the master doesn't place you above them right away. If he sees that you're a good worker, he'll know the right place for you.

Ask the companions if they're all going to the hostel and what a newcomer should contribute to the kitty. They'll instruct you... The elder will tell you: "A groschen or nine pence, according to custom." At the hostel the elder will say: "Here and elsewhere, it's the custom to meet at the hostel every fortnight and each one pays the week's dues." If your mother has furnished your purse well, take the money and fling it on the table so that it bounces into the elder's face, and say: "That's for me, give me my change." Is that what you'll do? A. Yes. Q. Oh, no. Take the money in your right hand, put it politely in front of the elder, and say: "With your permission, here's mine." Don't ask for change. The elder will know what change you're owed if you have given more than necessary... (Here one "planes" him for the third time.)

If the elder says to you, "Companion, for the pleasure of masters and companions, go and fetch some beer," don't refuse. If you run into a girl or a good friend, you'll give them some of your beer, you understand? A. Yes. Q. Oh, no. If you want to do someone a kindness, take your money and say: "Here, go drink to my health. When the companions have broken up, I'll come join you." Otherwise, they'll punish you. At the end of the meal, get up from the table and cry, "Fire!" The others will come to put it out...

The sponsor returns at this point and says: with your permission, masters and companions, I declare: I just brought you a *Goatskin*, a hoop-murderer, a slat-wrecker, a knockabout, traitor to masters and companions. Now I hope to bring you a solid, honest companion... My godson, I wish you happiness and prosperity in your new estate and on your travels. May God protect you on land and sea. If today or tomorrow you come to a place where the customs of the trade are no longer kept, work to restore them. If you don't have any money, try to earn some. Make the customs of the trade respected, don't let them be neglected. Introduce ten fine companions, wherever you can find them, sooner than a single bad one. If you can't find any at all, pick up your bundle and move on.

The apprentice must now run into the street crying, "Fire!" The companions come after him with a great dousing of cold water. Then comes the meal. They crown him, give him the place of honor, and drink his health.

To finish this introduction to the spirit of German companions let me introduce a number of their popular books, taken from Goerres, *Volksbücher*.

The Miller's Crown of Honor, revised and enlarged, or Complete Explanation of the true nature of the Circle, dedicated to the company of Millers by a miller's assistant called Georg Bohrmann, presented to his companions that they might remember him well. His verses and writings have been printed because, as Sirak says, one knows the artisan by his work. Printed in the current year. (This title is in verse.) Written in Meissen. The best book produced in Germany by the guild spirit—a spirit of calm and dignified simplicity; easy versification. The initial woodcut represents a circle with mystical sayings. The explanation that follows tells us that everything was created by the circle. In the second illustration, the author attempts to show us the world within the cross. There follows a history of the miller's profession according to Holy Scripture, then a satirical dialogue, a poetical voyage, and a description of the best mills in the Lausitz, Silesia, Moravia, Hungary, Bohemia, Thuringia, and Franconia; respects and good wishes for Nuremberg. In the form of a triangle, the names of the three best millers who ever were. The author concludes reverently with God, *the architect of the world*, and with praise of the miller's estate. A book known apparently only in north Germany.

Some fine new formulas of the honorable corps of Carpenters, customarily pronounced at the completion of a new building, when a bouquet or a wreath is hung in the presence of a number of spectators. Published for the first time in the current year. Cologne and Nuremberg. The house is considered to be the mystical image of the visible church. The ceremony for placing a bouquet on the completed house. The address to be delivered from the roof-ridge.

Customs of the honorable trade of Bakers, how each one should conduct himself at the hostel and at work. Printed as an aid for those about to go traveling. Nuremberg.

Origin, antiquity, and glory of the honorable company of Furriers. Exact description of all the formulas long observed in keeping with the statutes of the corporation in the engagement, initiation, and reception of a master, and of how one examines the companions. Faithfully described by Jacob Wahrmund [truthful mouth], *printed for the first time.* The furriers and tanners claim the distinction of having had God himself as their first companion, since it is written that God made coverings of skins for Adam and Eve — an honor unmatched by other companies. The companion must be a fully legitimate child.

The symbolic genius of the books of companionage contrasts with *Eulenspiegel,* the popular book of the German peasants.

Eulenspiegel [mirror of owls] *redivivus, surprising and marvelous history of Till Eulenspiegel, son of a peasant, born in Braunschweig, translated from the Saxon into good High German, revised and improved by several illustrations, a highly amusing work, followed by a comical addition: well embellished and reworked. Cologne and Nuremberg.* Spirit of great mischief — the spirit of the peasant of the north personified. Eulenspiegel frequents all the social classes, exercises every trade. This is the people's fool, by contrast with the princes' fools. The first edition appeared in 1483. During the Reformation, the Eulenspiegel of the fourth edition (Strassburg) was, like Germany itself, half Catholic, half Protestant. In the latter capacity, he makes fun of popes and priests. Translated into French, into Latin iambics, and later into many other languages. The book was a great success among the peasants of interior Switzerland, those robust mountain men whose flesh is so strong and powerful and who take no offense at the obscenities of Eulenspiegel. It is said that the hero really existed and died in 1350. His grave, they say, is pointed out under the lime trees at Moellen near Lübeck. The gravestone is said to bear a chiseled owl and a mirror. The owl signifies the mischievous, gluttonous, thieving character of Eulenspiegel.

Next to this national book stands the *History of Faust.* It is drawn from a larger work bearing the title: *First part of the horrible and abominable sins and vices, and of the amazing miracles, that Dr. Johannes Faustus, celebrated magician and arch-sorcerer, effected by his magic until he met a terrible end,* Hamburg, 1599. The depositions of a great number of eye witnesses prove the existence of Faust at the end of the fifteenth and beginning of the sixteenth century. A contemporary and a friend of Paracelsus and of Cornelius Agrippa, Faust is mentioned by Melanchton (in his letters), Conrad Gessner, and Manlius in *Collectaneis locorum communium.* Widmann cites Luther on the subject of Faust. The abbot Tritheim, in his private letters, treats him as a fool and an imposter: "Did he not dare to say that the books of Aristotle and of Plato, if they should all perish with their author, would be restored to the world by his genius, just as Esdras recovered the sacred books in his memory!" Every era had its Faust, to whom contemporaries always attributed something supernatural. All of these figures came together in the true and final Faust, who then became the chief of all previous sorcerers, perfected their great oeuvre, and did much else. Faust therefore is more a book than a person. Everything that his biography recounts about his feats of sorcery was transmitted by the tradition for centuries, and the image of Faust was merely imprinted like a seal on the universal collection. Widmann's piece is based on an autograph manuscript of Faust that the three sons of a famous doctor in Leipzig found in their father's library. The manuscript may well be by Waiger or Wagner, a disciple of Faust, who speaks of him in these terms: "Discreet, roguish and resourceful, smart enough, taken for mute at school with bakers and butchers, but a very good talker at home; a bastard, for all that." Faust made Wagner his heir, left him all his books, and said to him before his death: "I bid you not to reveal my art and my methods until long after my death. Then gather the facts carefully and write a history. Your familiar spirit, the heath cock, will help you with this labor and will remind you of what you may have forgotten. For people will want to know my history as you have recorded it."

The popular literature of Germany comes to an end with the Reformation, or rather, it all comes together in Luther himself, the most popular writer of all time. Just before that period (around 1500), two poets stand out, the shoemaker Hans Sachs and the imperial preacher Murner. I shall not discuss Sebastian Brant, adviser to Maximilian, author of the *Ship of Fools* (*Narrenschiff*), which had so little merit and has known so little success, and which perhaps served as a model for the *Emblemata* of Alciatus. Brant puts the friends of the printing press into the first rank of fools, saying that the press "will soon fall into disrepute."

Hans Sachs is more interesting. (See his works, reprinted at Nuremberg, 1781, 5 vols.; his life, by Ranisch; and the works of Wagenseil, Schoeber, Hirsch, Dunkel, Will, and Riederer.) His life, however uneventful, nonetheless shows the mores and the singular culture of German artisans of the time. He was born in 1494 to a tailor in Nuremberg, sent at seven to the Latin school, apprenticed at fifteen to a shoemaker, and traveled at seventeen to Regensburg, Passau, Salzburg, and Innsbruck, where he was retained as chasseur to Emperor Maximilian (*Unnutze Pflege der Frau*, vol. I of his works in the edition of 1590, and vol. IV, p. 294.) He then went to Munich, stopped at Wurzburg and at Frankfurt, then at Koblenz, Cologne, and Aachen. His master of poetry was Leonard Nunnenbek, a weaver at Nuremberg. On his travels he learned a great number of meters, and when he reached Upper Austria, he decided to devote his life to letters (*The Gifts of the Muses*, vol. II).[x] Shortly afterwards, he kept his first school at Frankfurt. After visiting Leipzig, Lübeck, Osnabruck, Vienna, and Erfurt, he returned to Nuremberg, aged 22 (1516), at his father's wish. Received as master shoemaker, he married in 1519, opened a small shop in a neighboring village, and returned shortly afterwards to the Frankfurt fair. He lived happily with his Kunegunde for more than forty years, had two sons and five daughters, who all predeceased him. He married again in 1561 (*Künstliches Frauenlob*, vol. V). He lost the use of his faculties at 76 and died at 82, in 1576.

In 1523 he produced a panegyric to the Reformation, *The Wittemberg Nightingale, which is now heard everywhere.*[xi] In the woodcut one sees a nightingale with the sun, moon, and various animals and, on a mountain, a lamb with a victory standard. At the very end: *Christus amator. Papa peccator.* One Father Spee published a refutation entitled *My Challenge to the Nightingale.* Hans Sachs also wrote prose dialogues on the subject of the Reformation, 1524. The first is entitled *Dispute between a Canon and a Shoemaker, wherein is defended the word of God and a Christian way of life. Hanus Sachs. MDXXIIII.* The engraving represents, among other figures, a shoemaker with a pair of house slippers in his hand.

The most curious of the works of Hans Sachs, which I shall summarize, is *A Short Humorous Carnival Skit for three characters, to wit: a burgher, a peasant, and a nobleman. The Empty Cakes* (ed. 1781, in-8, p. 290; ed. 1821, in-24, p. 161). The title is vague and the moral, placed at the end, has no connection with the skit. Perhaps the author found such precautions prudent for a work in which he gave the advantage to the peasant in the presence of the burghers of Nuremberg, at a time when the almost universal revolt of the German peasants was raising the most violent animosity against them. The play is not dated, contrary to the author's usual practice, but a reference to Goetz von Berlichingen, leader of the revolting peasants, indicates that it was probably composed after 1525.

The peasant wants to sit down beside the burgher and take part in the festivities; the burgher rejects him and insults him; the peasant then produces a burlesque genealogy and adds: "On my mother's side, I am a Goetz ('Goetz' for *Klotz*, a stump or block of wood). That's why those who know me call me Goetz Toelp Fritz. Now that you know who I am, consider me one of the guests and let me take a seat at table."

Burgher: Out of here, you idiot. Don't you see a nobleman coming? What are you doing here with us? *Nobleman:* What are you doing here, Toelp Fritz? Can't you find a hostel in the village without coming here with the burghers? *Burgher:* That's what I was telling him, chevalier. *Peasant:* May I tell you both what I think? *Nobleman:* Speak, Toelp, or you'll explode. You're a real peasant. *Peasant:* Anyone who opened the peasant veins that you have could easily bleed you to death. *Nobleman:* Do you hear this ass? Throw him down the stairs. *Peasant:* At least hear me out. Adam, says our priest, was the father of us all. We are all his children. *Nobleman:* True, but there's a difference. Noah had three sons. One was a rascal called Cham and was a peasant. The lines of the burghers and the noblemen descend from Sem and Japhet. *Peasant:* I've also heard tell that nobility comes from virtue, that in the old days the nobles protected widows and orphans and defended poor travelers. Is that still your custom, chevalier? *Nobleman:* Well, you tell me: wasn't it your custom in ancient times, you peasants, to be simple, just, and pious? Today you're nothing but rogues and scoundrels. You're hard-mouthed horses, you won't take the bit. And you—you're nothing but a boor. I am noble by birth. I can provide for myself without working; I have revenues and rents. I am polite and elegant when I go to the princes' court. *Peasant:* My kind of politeness is to work the land, sow, harvest, and thresh the grain, to cut hay, pull weeds, and all the other things I do to keep you both fed... Oh, well do I know how you live, both of you. Tell me, noble sir, your horse, when you're on the road, hasn't he ever bitten into a peddler's bag?

The peasant then demonstrates by hilarious proofs that he is happier than the nobleman and the burgher—something that real peasants would doubtless never have granted. Then many details follow concerning the curious customs of dress and games of the people and the diet of different classes of society. The nobleman is persuaded and says at last: "Egad, the peasant's right. Come, I'll celebrate carnival with you. We'll fill our glasses full, we'll drink, we'll gamble, and may the best man win." The burgher concludes:

Gentlemen, do not blame us if we have stopped too long with this crude peasant. He was as polite as he was able to be. As the saying goes, Put a peasant in a sack—his boots will always hang out. When you live among crude people, you become as crude as they are. Young people must therefore... etc. Hans Sachs wishes you Good Night.

Nothing is as unlike the genius of Hans Sachs as that of Murner. The shoemaker of Nuremberg always aims at elegance; he speaks of flowers and dells and often falls into triteness. Murner, learned man, preacher, poet laureate, affects crudeness to make himself understood by the people. His biting satires, *The Guild of Scoundrels* (*Schelmenzunft*) and *The Conspiracy of Fools* (*Narrenbeschwörung*), inspired by the corruption among the merchants of Strasbourg, are not at all reminiscent of Old Germany. We shall cite only the following passages:

"Some people want to decide what happens in the Empire, judge where the Emperor stands with Germany or with Italy, but on close inspection, no one has charged them with this task. *Who do the Venetians borrow from? How do they intend to sell? How does the pope keep up his household? Why does the Frenchman not remain in the alliance of the king of the Romans?* Whether we are eating or drinking, we deplore the power of that *sly fox* (Louis XII) *who wants to fool us. The king of Aragon does not want to pay the Venetians too handsomely. The Turks cross the sea, to our dismay, to say nothing of the cities of the Empire that did this and that to us, but they won't get away with it!* ...

"My dear friend, attend to your own business. Let the imperial cities be imperial cities. Have a glass of wine instead. It won't cost the Empire a single city... Have little and spend much, take the buttons off the noblemen's foils, fiddle secretly in one's coat, throw rocks through windows, write anonymous pamphlets, spread lies, disguise oneself in the priest's habit... Is it my fault that I mention these things here? I'm the current secretary of the *Scoundrels' Guild*. Let them choose somebody else."

PAGE 38. **Make himself the liege of another**... Is a vassal permitted to spit, cough, sneeze, or blow his nose in the presence of his lord? Should he not be punished for not having stood up straight, for having swung his sword around in his lord's presence? The *Jus feudale Alemanicum* asks these two questions. This dependency, servile in form, was usually ennobled by a sincerity of devotion that shows itself in touching fashion in these lines of Hartmann von Aue: "My joy was always uncertain until the day I gathered for myself the flowers of Christ that I now carry (insignia of the crusade). Since the day that death deprived me of my lord, he is the greater part of my joy, and half my pilgrimage is for him." Goerres, *Recueil des Minnesinger*, quoted from the preface.

Grimm (*Über den altdeutschen Meistergesang*, 1811) has amply established that the poet, like the knight, was the liege of the prince and lived from his lord's largesse. The poetry of praise, it seems, was a feudal service, like service in the military and at the bar. In the following verses a meistersinger undertakes to stir the generosity of the poor and chivalrous emperor Rudolf of Hapsburg by praise mixed with reproach:

"The king of the Romans gives nothing, and yet he is rich like a king; he gives nothing, but he is brave like a lion; he gives nothing, but he is very chaste; he gives nothing, but his life is irreproachable; he gives nothing, but he loves God and respects the virtue of women; he gives nothing, but never was a man more handsome; he gives nothing, but he is spotless; he gives nothing, but he is wise and pure; he gives nothing, but he judges fairly; he gives nothing, but he loves honor and fidelity; he gives nothing, but he is full of excellences. Alas! He gives nothing to anyone! What more shall I say? He gives nothing, but is a hero graceful and agile; he gives nothing, King Rudolf, whatever one may say or sing in his praise."

Page 39. *Frau...* the **Virgin**... It would be interesting to trace the long journey of the ideal of the Germanic woman from the ancient paganism of the North to the period of Christianity and chivalry, which placed her on the very altar and showed her transfigured at the right hand of God. At the outset, in the Nialsaga, woman has the beauty of a fierce purity; she is reared by a warrior who watches over her all his life and who kills pitilessly any mate wanting in respect for his daughter by adoption. Twice this fatal virgin thus costs her mate his life. In the Nibelungen, woman charms her barbarous lover as much by her strength as by her beauty.

"Various rumors arose on the Rhine; on the Rhine, it was said, there is more than one beautiful maiden. Mighty King Gunther wanted to obtain one of these and the desire grew and grew in his heart. There was a queen who had an empire by the sea; it was common knowledge that she had not her equal; she was immeasurably beautiful (*diu was unmazen schoene*) and her limbs were strong and powerful; she would challenge by javelin the swift warriors who quested after her love. She could throw a rock a great distance and recover it in a single leap. Whoever sought her love had to conquer the noble woman in three contests without blanching. If he was vanquished in a match, he paid with his head. A thousand times she had emerged from these contests still a virgin. On the Rhine a handsome hero heard these things and turned his thoughts to this beauty; the heroes, and he, paid with their heads.

"One day the king was in council with his men; they were considering which woman their master should make his wife and queen of a fine country. The chieftain of the Rhine then spoke: 'I want to go down to the sea, to Brunnhilde, whatever happens to me. For her love I shall risk my life and lose it if she is not my wife.' 'And I am going to dissuade you,' said Siegfried. 'That queen has barbarous customs. Anyone who pretends to her love plays for high stakes. For you on this quest I have frank and sincere advice.' 'Never was there a woman so strong and so bold,' said King Gunther. 'With my own hands I'll master her bodily in this contest.' 'Softly, softly; you don't know how strong she is. Even if you were a foursome, you'd not emerge safe and sound from her terrible rage. Renounce your wish, I advise you as a friend, and if you do not want to die, do not run such a horrible risk for her love.' 'Whatever her strength, I'll not renounce my quest. We'll go to Brunnhilde, whatever happens to me. For her prodigious beauty one must risk everything. Whatever God has in store for me, follow me to the Rhine.'" *Der Nibelungen Lied*, ed. 1820.

I have translated the passage in all its barbarous naiveté. It seems to me that Baron Eckstein, in his fine and eloquent translations from the Nibelungen published in *Le Catholique*, has softened its primitive, unpolished character, doubtless to accommodate the timidity of French taste.

Little by little the ideal of woman becomes more refined. Carnal woman carries the name WEIB, while spiritual woman, moral woman, sets herself apart from her as FRAU. One of the most celebrated meistersinger, Frauenlob, received his name for having maintained that distinction in many a poetic contest and for having celebrated in songs of love and in hymns by turns the ladies of this world and the ladies of paradise. Those of this world showed a tender appreciation toward this panegyrist of woman. They wanted to prepare the funeral celebration of their poet themselves. The stone of the sepulcher, to be seen still today in Mainz cathedral, represents them carrying the coffin of the man whom they inspired so long and whom they cost so many tears.

PAGE 39. **The Virgin**... See Grimm, *Altdeutsche Wälder*, introduction to "The Golden Forge" (a poem in honor of the Virgin) by Konrad von Würzburg, very interesting on account of the Christian myths of the Middle Ages. "One of the ideas that recurs most often among our meistersinger," the learned editor notes, "is the comparison of the incarnation of Jesus Christ with *the aurora of a new sun*. Every religion had its sun god, and since the fourth century the western church has celebrated the birth of Jesus Christ on the day the sun begins to climb again, on 25 December, that is to say, on the day one celebrated the birth of the *invincible sun*. There is an obvious connection with the sun god Mithra." (Creuzer, *Symbolik*, II, 220; Jablonski, *Opuscula*, III, 546 et seq.)

Our poets still say that Jesus lay at birth on the breast of Mary, like a bird that takes refuge at evening in a nocturnal flower that has opened on the high sea. What a remarkable connection with the myth of the birth of Brahma, enclosed in the water lily, the lotus, until the flower was opened by the rays of the sun, which is to say, by Vishnu himself, who had created that flower (see Mayer and Kanne[xii])! The Christ, the new day, is born of night, that is, of the Black Virgin, whose feet rest on the moon and whose head is crowned by planets in brilliant diadem (see the pictures by Albrecht Dürer).

Thus reappears, as in ancient cult, the great divinity variously called Maia Bhawani, Isis, Ceres, Proserpine, Persephone. Queen of the heavens, she is the night from which life emerges and to which all life returns—mysterious reunion of life and death. She is also called the dew, and in ancient German myth, dew represents the principle that reproduces and restores life. She is not only the night, but, as mother of the sun, also the dawn before which the planets shine and swarm, as they do for Persephone. When she signifies the earth as Ceres, she is represented carrying a wheat sheaf, just as Ceres wears a crown of wheat ears: she is Persephone, the seed grain. Like that goddess, she has a sickle, the half-moon lying beneath her feet. Finally, like the goddess of Ephesos, sorrowful Ceres and Proserpine, she is beautiful and brilliant and, at the same time, black and somber — in the words of the Song of Songs: "I am black and comely; the sun has burnt me"(Christ). Even today, the image of the mother of God is black at Naples and at Einsiedeln in Switzerland. Thus she combines day and night, joy and sorrow, sun and moon (warmth and moisture), the terrestrial and the celestial.

Page 39. **Flowers...** The minnesinger sing tirelessly of flowers and always begin by speaking of the beauty of the forests and their joyful music. After the example of the *Edda*, which so charmingly calls the winter "the mourning, suffering, and misery of the birds," one could group the subjects of most love songs into two classes, summer and winter: the joy, awakening, and life of the birds and flowers; the mourning, drowsiness, sleep and death of the flowers and birds. For the meanings of flowers and foliage, see Grimm, *Altdeutsche Wälder*, IV, after a fifteenth-century manuscript originally from Cologne, the Mosel valley, or perhaps from Flanders, Champagne, or Picardy, home of the *Rederiker* or Rhetors of the Middle Ages, who also often spoke of flowers. Here we find fixed positive rules about how lovers were to wear the foliage and flowers of their choosing or of their lady's bidding.

"*Oak.* One who wears oak leaves announces his strength and indicates that nothing can break his will. If he wears oak by order of his lady, it is a sign that no one should attack him, since oak is harder than any other wood. *Birch.* One who himself chooses a single master and willingly submits to his discipline, whether mild or harsh, may wear leafless birch; one who is ordered to wear birch is to understand that he will not be treated too rigorously, though he will still be kept under the lash. *Chestnut.* One who cherishes his beloved more and more each day and is pleasing to his lady may wear prickly chestnuts, the more prickly the better. *Heather.* One who chooses heather with its foliage and flowers shows that his heart loves solitude, like the heather, which likes to grow in barren places and does not live close to other plants. If he is ordered to wear heather, he is advised to love only his own lady, to keep watch on himself, and to exalt his love and joy, just as heather and its like climb up hills and rocks, though hardly noble of itself. *Bluet.* One whose flighty heart itself does not know where it should light and fix its constancy should wear bluets, a pretty blue flower which, however, fades and cannot keep its color. *Rose.* One who cherishes in his beloved innocence and a fear of sin, and who protects her from himself may wear a rose with its thorns."

Page 39. **Childlike and profound...** See the charming collection entitled *Des Knaben Wunderhorn (The Boy's Wondrous Horn)*. Most of these popular songs, so sweet, so inspired by calm and solitude, are as dear to my heart and as known to my ear as the most delicious cradle songs that I ever heard on my mother's knee. I would not dare attempt to translate any.

PAGE 39. **Wolfram's Parsifal**... Though it may cause the reader to smile, I will quote the entire passage on Parsifal in Grimm (*Altdeutsche Wälder*, I).

"The noble hero, whose youth, as simple and naïve as his childhood, is sheltered and watched over by an excessively timid mother, continues to resist the secret voice that summons him more insistently every day to the service of God. Stung by the reproach of Sigunen, Parsifal sets out over forests and wilderness for the city of miracles. At daybreak one morning, snow conceals his way; he rides through underbrush and over rocky outcroppings. Soon the white forest has become brilliant in the sunshine. He approaches a field where a flock of wild geese has just alighted. A falcon swoops down and attacks one of them, which takes flight. Three drops of blood fall from its wounds—an object of sadness for Parsifal and his love. When he sees these drops of blood on the pure white snow, he says to himself: 'Who has painted these vivid colors with such skill? Condviramurs, that color is like yours. God is protecting me; he wants me to see your image here. Praise be to God and all his creatures! Condviramurs, this is your coloring. The snow lends the blood its whiteness and the blood reddens the snow. It is the image of your lovely body.' The hero's eyes brim with tears; he remembers the day when two tears ran down Condviramurs's cheeks and a third down her chin. This secret comparison occupies him and absorbs him entirely; he is no longer aware of what is happening around him; he stands still in a dreamlike state as if he were asleep.

"A knight sent out to meet him calls to him, and he does not respond, does not move; and then he finds himself unhorsed. In getting up, he steps on the drops of blood and can no longer see them. At that point he comes to himself and unhorses his importunate enemy. Then, without a word, he returns to the drops of blood and contemplates them anew. A second horseman fares no better. The third is wiser: seeing that Parsifal does not respond to his polite, well-chosen greeting, he understands that he is in the thrall of love and searches for the object of his unwavering gaze. Then he takes a wildflower and lets it fall on the drops of blood. As soon as the flower has covered and concealed the droplets, the hero returns to himself and asks sorrowfully only who has snatched away his lady.

"This shows us in singular, touching fashion how much he loves the woman whom he himself had been willing to give up for the sake of God and chivalry. In the middle of a remote wilderness, a memory of her overtakes him suddenly like a painful dream from which only force can tear him away. At the same spot where he saw the droplets on the snow rises the tent where five years later he finds his beloved wife sleeping on her couch with infant twins whom he does not yet know. In the three drops of blood he had recognized the three tears that he saw on Condviramurs's face; he did not know that they foretold his wife with two infants in her arms, like three bright pearls...

"In the old French poem by Chrétien de Troyes, Gawain, the hero's friend, does not throw flowers on the drops of blood. The snow melts slowly in the sun. When two droplets have disappeared, Parsifal begins to emerge from his reverie. As the third disappears little by little, Gawain thinks it is time to greet him. This is the image of time, both kind and cruel, which, as peaceful as the sun, effaces, like the sun, the joys and sorrows of man."

There follows a reference to many passages on the opposition of red (birth), white (life, purity), and black (death).

PAGE 39. **With its immoral consequences.** In attacking these consequences and citing the threat to liberty in this doctrine, I am fully aware of its deeply poetic character. Undeniably, this wedding song of spirit and matter, of man and nature magnifies them, makes them magical, one by the effect of the other. "The divine spirit," Schelling says, "slumbers in the stone, dreams in the animal, and is awake in man." Man is the word of the world; since nature is aware of herself and recognizes her identity with him, he finds himself in all things and, in turn, feels the universe breathing in him; everywhere life reflects life. "Live not the stars and mountains? Are waves/ Without a spirit? Are the dropping caves/ Without a feeling in their silent tears?" (Byron)[xiii] When one passes through forests and wild valleys preoccupied with these ideas, it is such a sweetness, a mystical sensuality to add to one's own being the air, the waters, the green world, or rather, to let one's personality go in avid nature, which draws it to her and seems to want to absorb it. The voice of the siren is so sweet that you would follow it, like Goethe's fisherman, down into the deep, clear spring or, like Empedocles, to the bowels of Etna. *O mihi tum quam molliter ossa quiescant!*

It is a marvelous thing how that doctrine has taken possession of dreamy Germany and infiltrated all her literature. You will find its influence in nearly every book, in art, criticism, philosophy, and song. I know one student song, very beautiful, but I prefer to cite the following, composed in France during the war of 1815. Amid the ardor of youth and the exaltation of combat, a philosophical turn of thought occurs willy-nilly.

"Nothing in the world is more gay, more swift than are we, the hussars on the battlefield. Lightning flashes, thunder rumbles; red as flame, we fire at the foe; blood courses in our eyes; we make hail. They call to us: 'Hussars, fire your pistols, strike, saber in hand, split the man before you.' You don't know French? Don't let that bother you! He'll speak his language no more when you cut off his head. If a loyal comrade remained on the field, the hussars would not mourn. The body rots in the grave, the uniform stays in the world, the soul is exhaled into air, under the deep blue dome."

PAGE 40. **A wood, a meadow, a spring.** Ne pati quidem inter se junctas sedes. Colunt discreti ac diversi; ut fons, ut campus, ut nemus placuit, etc. Tacitus, *Germania*, XVI.

PAGE 40. **Our good Nuremberg...** The custom of decorating house fronts with fine quotations from the scriptures is practiced throughout Germany. I cite Nuremberg because it has preserved its ancient aspect like no other city. It is the Pompeii of the Middle Ages.

PAGE 40. **Stags coming to drink under the balconies of electors.** Here I have yielded to a two-fold temptation: to the pleasure of mentioning the charming small town of Heidelberg, which leaves its visitors with so many memories and such longing, and to that of mentioning it in the terms of a great writer who is very dear to me, the translator of Herder and author of *Voyage en Grèce*, Edgar Quinet.

PAGE 40. **How many times has Germany not risen, only to fall back again...** There is no more faithful image of this than the Rhine. A true symbol of the genius of that land, it reflects German history just as well as it does the trees and rocks of its banks. It rises from the depths of the Alps in a torrent and drowses again at Lake Constance. It surges once more over a bed broken by rock, rages and falls furiously at Schaffhausen, making both Swabia and Switzerland tremble. Never fear. It settles again and rolls, wide and deep as the Nibelungen, whose theater it crosses. Narrow again at Bingen, the heroic river cuts its way between basalt giants, past all the castles that command its banks and sometimes seem to have come down, armed to the teeth, to block its passage (in the Palatinate).

Finally, when it has paid its respects to the never-to-be-finished cathedral of Cologne, weary of these noble efforts and disillusioned, it saunters past the prosaic flats of the Low Countries and if any reverberation is heard along its banks it is of a declamation by a Flemish Rederiker, the monotonous song of a Baenkelsaenger, a singing smith or carpenter hammering at his work from Cologne to Holland. Thus the Rhine reaches the ocean, into which it vanishes without regret. This too is an image of Germany resigned to being absorbed into Schelling's absolute unity. Content to come to rest in infinity, she sounds one last poetic chord in Goethe and Goerres.

PAGE 40. **In Iceland the gods will die like us**... See Geiers, *Schwedens Geschichte*. Only one volume has been translated into German as yet. I also eagerly await the publication of J.-J. Ampère's important work, *La Littérature du Nord*. Prepared by much travel and deep, wide-ranging study, it will reveal a whole new world to the French public.

PAGE 41. **In Luther's lifetime, at his very table, began the mysticism**... Luther is little known. Bull-necked, of choleric aspect (see the fine portraits by Lucas Cranach), furiously violent in his style, he was, for all that, a gentle soul, very receptive to music, as responsive to friendship as he was to love. Nothing pained him more than to see his most cherished disciples, guests in his house, abandon his teachings, or rather, take them rigidly to their logical extreme. In his attacks on Rome he had written: "Let law perish and grace live!" After that, had he any right to complain that the Lutherans were disposed toward mysticism? In the first half of his life, he too had been prodigiously mystical.

PAGE 41. **That would triumph in Boehme**... A shoemaker in Goerlitz, died 1624. Saint-Martin has translated three of his works: *L'Aurore naissante*, *Les Trois Principes*, and *La Triple Vie* or *L'Éternel Engendrement sans origine*, 1802. He undertook to translate all fifty volumes of Boehme. Many passages by this theosophist are highest poetry, for example, the entire beginning of the second volume of *Les Trois Principes*.

I would not conclude these notes on Germany without citing certain observations by Mme de Staël, striking in their aptness and insight. They apply to contemporary German society, yet are marvelously confirmed by the ancient literature of this people, which the author did not know.

"There is a certain physical well-being that turns one's thoughts to sensations in the south of Germany and to ideas in the north. Vegetative existence in the south of Germany corresponds in some ways to contemplative existence in the north: there is repose, idleness, and reflection in both."

"Tyrolean farce, which amuses both the nobility and the people in Vienna, is much more akin to the buffoonery of the Italians than to the mockery of the French."

"In Germany, anyone who does not concern himself with the universe has nothing to do."

"For the superior men of the respective countries to attain the highest degree of perfection, the Frenchman must become religious and the German a bit worldly."

"There is more sensibility in English poetry and more imagination in German poetry. The Germans, being more independent in all things because they do not carry the imprint of any political institution, depict the sentiments as they depict ideas: through a scrim. One could say that the universe shimmers before their eyes and the very uncertainty of their gaze multiplies the number of objects that their talent can make use of."

"Among the Latin nations one has often seen a politics singularly adroit in the art of escaping one's obligations; the German nation, be it said to its credit, is almost incapable of this barefaced deviousness, which will bend any verity for the sake of interest and sacrifices every kind of engagement to calculated advantage."

"Tile stoves, beer and tobacco smoke build a kind of dense, warm atmosphere around the popular classes in Germany, from which they do not like to emerge. When the climate is only half rigorous and it is still possible to escape the insults of the heavens by means of household measures, those measures themselves make men more sensitive to the physical sufferings of war."

"Imagination, which is the dominant quality of Germany, both artistic and literary, inspires a fear of danger, unless the force of opinion and an exaltation of honor combat this natural reaction."

"The French, quite unlike the Germans, consider actions with the liberty of art and ideas with the servitude of custom."

"Since the Germans have more imagination than true passion (in matters of love), the most bizarre events take place there in a curious tranquility. And yet it is thus that custom and character lose all firmness. A spirit of paradox shakes the most sacred institutions and there are no fixed rules in any matter."

ITALY

PAGE 41. **Italy can plead the languor of the climate, the disproportionate forces of the conquerors, etc.** But the best excuse of this unhappy land is that its fatal beauty has always aroused the desires and the brutal love of all the barbarian peoples. The icy giants that nature placed at its portals, as if for defense, have served for nothing. The conquerors have never been deterred by the extreme difficulty of passage. Only recently, one still descended Mount Cenis by a slope so rapid that it carried the traveler's sledge a distance of two leagues in ten minutes.

One may cross the Alps from the side, either through Savoy or through Germany, or one may go through the center of Switzerland. This last passage, the Simplon, is short and abrupt. From the gloomy Valais, where you leave behind the men of the North and the chalets of painted wood, you drop down into Milan amid noise, brilliant light, and Italian bustle, among orange trees and houses of marble. The Simplon is the triumphal entry into Italy. The artist and the poet will choose this route. The historian will prefer to enter from the east or from the west; these are effectively the two routes that the armies and the great emigrations have followed. The Gauls, Hannibal, Bonaparte, countless French armies went by Mt. Cenis or the St. Bernard; the Goths of Alaric and Theodoric, the Germans of Othon the Great, of Frederick Barbarossa, and of so many emperors entered by the defiles of Tyrol.

Even today, when one sees the terrible barrier of the Alps, one shudders to think what men once risked and suffered in order to penetrate into this garden of the Hesperides. Hannibal entered the Alps with 50,000 men and emerged with 25,000. No matter: all the nations of the world by turns have wanted to pitch their tents on that ground, to enjoy its fruits and its skies, even at the price of being buried there. The Gauls were in search of the vine, the Normans of the lemon tree. There Louis XII and Francis I consumed their lives and their subjects to regain "their lovely betrothed," as they called Naples and Milan. The Goths thought they would find their Asgard here, the mysterious and much blessed city from which they said their ancestors had been exiled. Alaric claimed that an invisible fatality was drawing him toward Rome and that he would die on leaving it.

Effectively, nature has laid invincible seductions upon that land. "I feel sure," Goethe says in his memoirs, "that I was born there and that I am returning after a whale hunt that took me to Greenland": *Kennst du das Land, wo die Zitronen blühn,* etc. (Goethe, *Wilhelm Meister*)[xiv]

Another of the seductions of Italy is that peril there lies close to pleasure almost everywhere. You have only just escaped glaciers and avalanches when you come upon the Borromean isles and the magic of Lago Maggiore. The fertile plains of the Po are only just protected, by dikes, from the incursions of the most impetuous of rivers. The Tuscan maremma and the Roman campagna are as notable for their murderous insalubrity as for their fertility. "In the maremma," goes a Tuscan proverb, "one becomes rich in a year's time and one dies in six months." On Vesuvius, see my *Histoire Romaine*, ch. 2.

Page 41. **The Italian makes God come down to him, seeks here an objet d'art.** And even in the ceremonies of religious observance he often succeeds in doing this with admirably dramatic genius. At the feast of the Assumption in Messina, the Virgin is carried all through the city in search of her son, just as the goddess of ancient Sicily searched for Proserpine. Finally, at the moment when she is about to enter the central square, she comes face-to-face with the image of the Savior. She trembles and draws back in surprise, and twelve birds fly from her bosom, carrying her burst of maternal joy toward God. How could cruel Mr. Blunt have seen in this nothing more than ridiculous mummery? (*Vestiges of Ancient Manners and Customs discoverable in modern Italy and Sicily*, by the reverend John James Blunt, fellow of St. John's College, Cambridge, and later one of the travelling bachelors of that university. London, J. Murray, 1823, p. 158.)

Page 42. **The prayers and formulas of augury are veritable contracts with the gods...** In the inscriptions one reads: "Aedem tempestatibus dedit *merito*... Pompeius votum *merito* Minervae." *Solvere vota* indicates discharge of a contractual obligation. The formula of the vow of a *ver sacrum* (Livy, XXII) and the formula of the consul Licinius against Antiochus (Livy, XXXVI) are veritable contracts with Jupiter.

Servius ad Aen. III (*ad versum*: Da, pater, augurium). *Legum dictio* apellatur, cum condictio ipsius argurii certa nuncupatione verborum dicitur, quali conditione augurium peracturus sit... tunc enim quasi *legitimo* jure *legem* adscribit.

Varro has preserved the augural formula by which the site of the Capitol was chosen (in my *Histoire Romaine*, Book I).

Page 42. **To find the finest fruits, to recover a lost bird...** Cicero, *De Divinatione*. For those Romans, famous for their gravity, therefore, religion was often an object of as little seriousness as it is for the Italians of today.

Page 42. **The popes were legists... "better than you men of law."** Expression by Philip of Valois, who sent the decision of the University of Paris on a question of dogma to Pope John XXII in 1333: "Mandans sibi a latere, quatenus sententiam magistrorum de Parisiis, qui melius sciunt quid debet teneri et credi in fide quam juristae et alii clerici, qui parum aut nihil sciunt de theologia, approbaret, etc." *Cont. chron.* Guil. de Nangis, p. 97. According to Pierre d'Ailly (*Concil. Eccl. Gall.*, 1406), the king went further; he ordered that the pope, who favored the opinion condemned by the university, be told: "qu'il se révoquast, ou qu'il le feroit ardre."

Page 42. **Pontifex...** "Pontifices ego a ponte arbitror; nam ab iis Sublicius est factus primum et restitutus saepe, cum ideo sacra et ultra et cis Tiberim non mediocri ritu fiant." Varro, *De Lingua latina*, IV, 15.

PAGE 42. **Etruscan monuments...** See the great work of Inghirami, the Atlas of Micali (*L'Italia Avanti*, etc.); Otfried Müller, *Die Etrusker*, etc.[xv]

PAGE 42. **Many churches, but these were the venues of political assemblies.** And the scene of countless political crises. Giuliano de' Medici and Gian Galeazzo Sforza were stabbed in churches. Among other passages that make the political character of the medieval churches vivid, see in our own Villehardouin the admirable scene where the ambassadors of the crusades implore, on their knees and in tears, aid for the people of Venice gathered in Saint Mark's. One could also cite any number of passages in Villani. The Duomo of Pisa, Santa Maria del Fiore at Florence, and all the old Italian churches that I recall have no tribune, because from a tribune one would have dominated the assembly of the sovereign people.

PAGE 42. **Strasbourg architects to close the vaults of the Milan cathedral.** The autograph letter exists, dated 1481. See Fiorillo, I.[xvi]

PAGE 42. **Never the very essence of feudalism, one man's pledged faith to another.** See, in Roman history and in medieval times, how readily clients and vassals turn against their patrons and their lords.

PAGE 42. **It knows how to die... but to die for an idea.** I cannot refrain from offering here the admirable account of the murder of Galeazzo Sforza (see Sismondi, *Rép. it.*, vol. XI, ch. 84, at year 1476), which was dictated between interrogation and torture by the young Girolamo Olgiati, one of those who committed the act. The Milanese could no longer endure this execrable tyrant, who took pleasure in having his victims buried alive and in letting them die slowly, fed only on human excrement. Three young men, Olgiati, Lampugnani, and Visconti (who was a priest), swore to avenge the insults they had suffered and to deliver their fatherland. Their first meeting took place in the garden of the basilica of Saint Ambrose.

"I then went into the church and threw myself at the feet of the statue of the holy pontiff with the following prayer: 'Great Saint Ambrose, keeper of this city, hope and defender of the people of Milan, if the undertaking that your fellow citizens have planned in order to expel tyranny, impurity, and monstrous debauchery is worthy of your approbation, favor us amid the dangers we incur in order to deliver our land.' After praying, I returned to my companions and exhorted them to take courage, assuring them that I felt full of hope and strength since I had invoked the protection of the patron saint of our homeland. In the following days we trained in fencing with daggers to acquire greater agility and to accustom ourselves to the perilous prospect before us... At the sixth hour of the night before Saint Stephen's

Day, our designated day to execute our plan, we met once more, expecting never to meet again. We chose the hour, the role of each of us, all the details of execution, to the extent that one could anticipate them. Early the following morning we went to Saint Stephen's and entreated the saint to favor the great deed that we were about to accomplish in his sanctuary and not to take offense if we should defile his altars with blood, since that blood was intended to deliver the city and the fatherland. After the prayers in the missal of that first martyr, we recited another that Carlo Visconti had composed. Then we attended the mass celebrated by the arch-priest of the basilica, and I requested the keys to the residence of that priest, to which we retired."

The conspirators were gathered around the fire in that house because fierce cold had driven them from the church, when the noise of the crowd announced the approach of the prince. It was the day after Christmas, 26 December 1476. Galeazzo seemed to be kept back by presentiment: he had decided to leave the house only reluctantly. He now proceeded to the festival, flanked by the ambassadors of Ferrara and of Mantua. Inside the church Gian-Andrea Lampugnani advanced toward him until he reached the Rock of the Innocents, parting the crowd with his hand and his voice. When he stood before him, he laid his left hand, as if with respect, on the toque that Galeazzo held in his hand; he dropped to one knee, as if to present a petition, and with his right hand holding a short dagger that he had concealed in his sleeve, he slit the duke's belly from bottom to top. Simultaneously, Olgiati attacked his chest and throat, and Visconti his shoulder and the middle of the back. Sforza fell into the arms of the two ambassadors who accompanied him, crying: "Oh, God." The blows were struck so quickly that the ambassadors themselves did not yet know what had happened. At the moment when the duke was killed, violent disorder broke out in the church. A number of men pulled their swords; some fled, others came running up. No one yet knew the aim of the conspirators or their number. But the guards and the courtiers who recognized the murderers set out in pursuit. In attempting to leave the church, Lampugnani plunged into a group of kneeling women and caught his spurs in their robes; he fell and a Moorish groom of the duke overtook him and killed him. Visconti was stopped shortly afterward and also killed by the guards. Olgiati escaped from the church and appeared before his own door, but his father would not receive him and closed the house against him. A friend gave him refuge, where he was not safe for long. He was, as he says himself, about to leave the house and to rally the people to a freedom that the Milanese no longer knew, when he heard a raging mob as it came dragging the broken body of his friend Lampugnani through the muddy streets. He froze in horror, lost courage, and waited for the fatal moment when he would be found. He was put to terrible torture. His body broken, his joints dislocated, he composed the detailed account required of him, which has come down to us. He ends with these words: "And now, holy mother of our Lord, and you, O Princess Bona [the widow of Galeazzo], I beg that your goodness and mercy provide for the salvation of my soul. I ask only that one leave enough life in this miserable body to let me confess my sins in keeping with the rites of the Church and then to undergo my fate."

Olgiati was twenty-two years old at the time. He was condemned to be tortured with hot pincers and to be dismembered alive. In the midst of these atrocious torments, a priest exhorted him to repent. Olgiati replied: "I know that I have deserved these torments by many errors, and worse, if my feeble body could support them. But as for the noble feat for which I must die, it reassures my conscience: far from believing that I have deserved my punishment by it, I place in it my hope that the supreme judge will pardon my other sins. No culpable cupidity led me to that deed, only the desire to remove from our midst a tyrant whom we could no longer endure. If I should be revived ten times to die again ten times in the same torment, I would nonetheless dedicate all my blood and all my strength to an end so noble." The executioner, ripping his skin from his chest, caused him to cry out, but he quickly recovered his composure. "This death is hard," he said in Latin, "but the glory of it is eternal!" *Mors acerba, fama perpetua; stabit vetus memoria facti.* (*Confessio Hieronymi Olgiati morientis,* apud Ripamontium, *Historiae ecclesiae mediolanensis,* I, 6, p. 649.)

Page 43. **Genius passionate but stern... artificial world of the city.** I am aware of the objections that can be raised in light of the present state of Italy. But my task here is to characterize each people by the whole of its development and its history. Even today everything I describe exists, if one does not see all of Italy in terms of Florentine sweetness, Milanese sensuality, and the languor of the Bay of Naples.

Page 43. **Indestructible Roman law...** One sees in the third volume of Gans (*Erbrecht*) how forcefully that law combated the spirit of the Goths, the Lombards, and the Franks. The influence of the popes themselves modified it less than one would like to believe. This ingenious author remarks that Catholicism in Italy is like a duomo that can be seen throughout the land, toward which one turns to pray but which one does not notice when one is busy with other things. The work being prepared by M. Forti (of Florence) will show us still more completely how this particularly Italian form of Roman law developed in the Middle Ages. I have the greatest hopes of the efforts of this knowledgeable young jurisconsult. Not for nothing does one carry in one's veins the blood of the Sismondi.

PAGE 43. **Cardano and Tartaglia... Campanella and the unfortunate Bruno.**
Nowhere has destiny been more cruel toward genius than in Italy. This is explained
by the contradiction of a strong personality injured and broken under the yoke of
the citadel or of the church. The misfortunes of Dante are known to us, as is the
inelegant, painful epitaph that he himself composed for his tomb at Ravenna:

> Hic condor Dantes, patriis extorris ab oris,
> Quem genuit parvi Florentia mater amoris.

All the great men of Italy have come to know, as he did, what it is to *go up and
down the stranger's stair and to taste how salty is the bread of other people.* Campanella,
that heroic monk who wanted to arm all the monasteries of Calabria and who
negotiated with the Turks to deliver his land from the Spanish, spent twenty-seven
years in a dungeon. The sonnets he composed there, which we have today, show
just how powerless captivity was to break his spirit. He managed to recover his
freedom, took refuge in France, and died there a friend of Cardinal Richelieu, who
often came to consult him in his cloister in the rue Saint-Honoré.

Tartaglia received this ridiculous name ("the Stammerer") because at age twelve
he was slashed by the French at the sack of Brescia, in a church where his mother
had sought asylum. The blow split his lip; if it had struck higher, that would have
been the end of the restorer of mathematics.

Cardano, among other misfortunes, knew that of seeing his son executed for
murder by poison. The life of this extraordinary man, which he wrote himself, is
inferior in style, but not in the interest of its psychological observations, to the
Confessions of Saint Augustine, of Montaigne, and of Rousseau.

What can one say of the painful life and horrible death of poor Giordano Bruno?
One cannot see without emotion the sweet and suffering face (at the beginning of
the *Life* by Silber and Rixner) of this man who was tracked through all Europe like a
wild beast. After wandering from Geneva to Wittenberg and from Paris to London,
this poor Italian wanted to see once more the sun of his own country and let himself
be seized at Venice. We know that he was condemned as an atheist at Rome and
died at the stake. One could criticize an immoral tendency in his doctrine, but how
can he be accused of atheism? This "atheist" has left us countless religious poems,
among other things a lovely sonnet, in the manner of Petrarch, *to love.* By this he
always means divine love.

PAGE 43. **Venetian palette, Lombard grace**... Lombardy, Celtic by origin and
situated between France and Italy, between movement and beauty, expresses itself in
painting by *the beauty of movement,* by grace. The Venetian school is distinguished by

its palette, the Florentine and Roman schools by design. Thus painting, proceeding from Venice to Naples, loses its concrete character and spiritualizes itself, to coin a phrase. It reaches its highest degree of abstraction and spiritualization in Salvator Rosa. The paintings of this great artist have neither brilliance of color nor severity of design, but they are full of life and of ingenious touches. The school of Bologna, coming after all the others, shows an admirable eclecticism.

Italian art early lost its symbolic genius, smothered practically at birth by a feeling for form, by an adoration of physical beauty. Germany, by contrast, sees in art only symbolism; wholly dedicated to idea, it makes form accessory. Thus the honest ugliness present almost everywhere in German art; but the charm of its moral beauty is often so affecting that the soul denies the judgment of the eyes. When Germany unites idea and form, it equals or surpasses Italy. Who can decide between the Virgins of Cologne and those of the Campo Santo of Pisa?

No memory and no regret of Italy has remained more vivid for me than that of the city of Pisa. Florence is quite splendid and Rome quite majestic and tragic, but, for all that, I think it would be sweet to live and die at Pisa and to sleep in the Campo Santo. Not only, I avow, because its earth was brought from Jerusalem by I know not how many galleys; but also because that Arab architecture is so weightless, those black and white marbles are in such sweet harmony, by their shadings into yellow, with the sky and the greensward; and that marble tower leans with such a compassionate air over the poor little old town, which has preserved nothing else of its one-time splendor. Ah! Those stones have feeling, have life. In the cloister, where so many mystic faces observed me with a critical eye, I noticed, among the ancient Etruscan tombs and those of Italian crusaders, the pensive statue of the German Henry VII, the chivalrous and devout emperor who was poisoned at communion and chose to die rather than reject the host.

PAGE 43. **The *agrimensor* and the haruspex measured and mapped the open fields... the jurist and the military strategist...** See my *Histoire* and the collection by Goesius.[xvii] In the judgment of Sulla himself, Marius was one of the most skillful farmers on earth.

PAGE 43. **The Italian gives his name to his estate.** Villae Tullianae at Tusculum, Formies, Arpinum, Calvi, Puteoli, Pompeii, etc. Today the ruins of these villas of Cicero are a subject of diligent research. The Villa Manzoni will excite the interest of future travelers no less.

PAGE 44. **The founders of military architecture...** Castriotto and Felice Paciotto, of the duchy of Urbino, who built the famous citadels of Antwerp and of Turin.

The classic work on military architecture by the Bolognese Marchi is well known. Another Bolognese, Antonio Alberti, was the first to think of the cadastre.

Page 44. **Judge France by the *canuts* of Lyon.** The name given in that city to the degenerate race that vegetates among its manufactures, particularly of silk.

Page 44. **The continuity of the Italian genius from ancient to modern times** ... See on this subject the work of Blunt, cited above, and that of Carlo Denina (Milan, 1807, in-8). Relevant also is the letter of Dr. Middleton following *La Conformité des Cérémonies* by P. Mussard (Amsterdam, 1744, 2 vols. in-12).

Page 45. **The national costume is almost the same**... Juvenal, *Sat.*, XIV, 186; III, 170; Plin., *Hist. N.*, IX, p. xxiii, 1. **Narrow streets.** Juv., III, 236. **Prandium at midday, the siesta, and the evening promenade.** Suet., *Aug.*, 78; Plin. Jun., *Epistulae*, III, 5; Plin., *Hist. N.*, VII, 44; X, 8; Mart., VI, 77, 10; Suet., *Aug.*, 43; Colum. praef.

Page 45. **The improviser... whether he is called Statius or Dante or Sgricci**... Juven., VII, 85. One still points out the stone opposite the cathedral of Florence where Dante would sit down among the people (*Sasso di Dante*). I resent those who set that venerable stone among the flags of a walkway: one must step aside to avoid treading on it. Dante, like Petrarch, declaimed his verses on the *Poggio imperiale* at the city gate toward Rome.

Page 45. **The *filosofi* of Venice... the open-air *literati*.** F.J.L. Meyer, *Darstellungen aus Italien*, 1784-85? Suet., *De Ill. Gr.*; Aul. G., II, 5.

Page 45. **The plow is the one that Virgil describes**... *Incumbere aratro* has always been the practice. A medal by Enna shows the plowman standing on a plank over the plowshare to impose his weight (*Hunter's Medals*, plate 25).

Page 45. **The savage type of the Bruttians**... *Séjour d'un officier français en Calabre*, 1820, p. 242. If we are to believe the witness of the Count of Zurlo, cited by Niebuhr, Greek is still spoken today in the area around Locrum. It is well understood that these are not Albanian colonies.

Page 45. **In the south, idealism, speculation, and the Greeks; in the north, sensualism, action, and the Celts**... See, below, one of the notes on France. The Italians are reproached, among other things, for being noisy and big talkers. This would be applicable only to the Italians of the north and of the south, i.e., to the Celts of Lombardy and the Greeks of the kingdom of Naples.

Page 45. **Bergamo, home of Harlequin**... Harlequin and Pulcinella have claim to an antiquity remote indeed if it is true that altogether analogous figurines have been found in Etruscan tombs.

Page 45. **The mysterious name of Rome**... The mysterious name of Rome was *Eros* or *Amor*; the sacerdotal name was *Flora* or *Anthusa;* the civil name was *Roma.* See Plin., *H. N.,* III, 5; Frederik C.C.H. Münter, "De occulto urbis Romae nomine," no. I of his *Antiquarische Abhandlungen* (Copenhagen, 1816).

Page 46. **Questa provincia pare nata a risuscitare le cose morte**... Machiavelli, *Arte della Guerra,* L, VIII, subfin.

Page 46. **Rome's sole export is earth itself, rags, and antiquities**... I refer to the pozzolana, which is sought from afar at Rome and used to make a durable cement. Rags are also exported in quantity and used in winter to wrap tender saplings, vines, and orange trees. As for antiquities, Rome has a market to which peasants come on an appointed day to sell what they have dug up during the week. Medals, figurines, etc., are sold there like fruits, vegetables, and other products of the soil.

Page 46. **The praetor and the tribune collecting the *sportula* from door to door**... This, as is known, was the basket of foodstuffs that the grandees of Rome had distributed at their gates to the clients who came to greet them. See Martial, III, 7, 2; Suet., *Claud.,* 32, and the fine passage from Juvenal:

> Nunc sportula primo
> Limine parva sedet, turbae rapienda togatae
> Ille tamen faciem prius inspicit, et trepidat ne
> Suppositus venias, ac falso nomine poscas.
> Agnitus accipies; jubet a praecone vocari
> Ipsos Trojugenas, nam vexant limen et ipsi
> Nobiscum: da Praetori, da deinde Tribuno.
> Sed libertinus prior est: prior, inquit, ego adsum, etc.

Page 46. **The staple food is still pork**... Polybius already speaks of the great number of pigs being raised in Italy, "whether for ordinary consumption or as provisions for war" (lib. II). The meat later distributed to the people was furnished by herds of pigs for whose fodder the emperors reserved the oak forests of Lucania.

Page 46. **Bullfights.** Only in Rome, in Spoleto, and in the Romagna does the people take pleasure in bullfights. They are unknown in Naples, despite the long presence of the Spanish. I note in passing that in Naples, for all its corruption, murder is as rare as it is common in Rome. Naples still has something of the gentleness of its Greek descent.

PAGE 46. **A knife thrust is a frequent, natural gesture in Rome**... An abbot kills a man; the people exclaim: *Poverino! Ha ammazzato un uomo!* Their compassion is with the murderer. After a festival, Meyer found 160 men with knife wounds at La Consolazione.

PAGE 46. **Death to my lord abbot**... "Che la bella principezza sia ammazzata! Che il signore abate sia ammazzato!" **And kings among the crowd**... I am speaking not only of illustrious travelers, like the present king of Bavaria and many others, but also of the kings living in Rome: of Christina, the Stuarts, Prince Henry of Prussia, the Napoleons. Rome is still a place of refuge. The churches are open to receive brigands, as in the asylum of Romulus. An encounter with a cardinal saves a condemned man, as in ancient times an encounter with a Vestal... **The air of that city carries a whiff of something stormy, frenzied, and immoral**... Hoffmann made Rome the setting of some of his tales.

PAGE 47. *Urbanitas*... **Emptiness of the environs of Rome**... **War feeding on itself**... See on all these matters my *Histoire Romaine*. **Caesar already was charged with draining the Pontine Marshes**. (Dion. Plut. Suet., 44). Cicero makes fun of the undertaking (*Philip.* 3).

To conclude these parallels between ancient and modern Italy, I add a few details on certain persistent beliefs. The people of the Roman campagna still fear the sorceress Circe and do not dare enter the cave of Circeio (Bonstetten, *Voyage sur le théâtre de l'Énéide*). The Romans are perfectly certain that bella Tarpeia lives at the bottom of an ancient well on the Capitoline, seated and covered with diamonds (Niebuhr). I confess that I searched there in vain for both the well and the tradition. All the Sabelli, especially the Marsi, interpreted omens, particularly the flight of birds. The Marsi charmed serpents and healed their bite. Still today jongleurs come to Rome and to Naples from the same countrysides. The Giravoli from the environs of Syracuse claim, like the ancient Psylli, to cure snakebite by their saliva. Like the statues of Eskapuleios and Hygieia, they carry a serpent in their hands. The people of the kingdom of Naples today attribute to San Domenico di Cullino what their ancestors attributed to Medea (Micali, *Italia*, etc., and Grimaldi, *Annali del R. di Napoli*, IV, p. 328. 38).

In ancient Rome, 420 temples; in modern Rome, more than 150 churches. The temple of Vesta is today the church of the Madonna del Sole; the temple of Romulus and Remus has become the church of Saints Cosmas and Damian, the twin brothers. It is believed that the temple of Salus has given way to San Vitale. Near Lavinium (Pratica) stands the chapel of Santa Anna Petronilla, on the very shore of the Nimicius from which Anna Perenna, the sister of Dido, hurled herself; she returned in the form of an old woman to feed the Roman people on the Mons Sacer. In the Forum Boarium, near the square of the Ara Maxima, where oaths were sworn (Mehercle), stands the church of Santa Maria in Cosmedin, better known to the people as Bocca della Verità.

Page 47. **The German, or Ghibelline, party...** If a Guelph wants to make himself a tyrant, Matteo Villani observes, he must switch and become a Ghibelline.

Page 48. **The radicalism of the Roman church...** I hope one day to prove and clarify what I content myself with merely stating here.

Page 48. **Local influences of race and climate...** It was Dr. Edwards, I believe, who first fully elucidated the fruitful principle of the persistence of race. I hope that this illustrious physiologist will eventually lay out his ideas on the crossing of races more extensively. He alone perhaps is capable of raising that particular part of physiology to the level of science, because he alone will take account of an element that has been too much neglected by those who address themselves to these studies. A combination of anatomy and chemistry is not yet physiology. The very same elements produce different products; the mystery of basic life, of life itself, introduces infinite variation into the outcomes. The combination of hydrogen and carbon produces both oil and sugar. From the Celto-Latino-Germanic mélange come both France and England.

FRANCE

Page 50. **The originalities of the provinces...** I have always been much affected by the sight of the endlessly renewed generations that my teaching brings before me every year. They soon escape me again and go their way, but each one leaves some interesting recollection. This sight was particularly striking at the École Normale. These students, coming from every province and so naively representing their types, offered in the aggregate a synopsis of France. It was then that I began to understand better the diverse nationalities of which the nationality of my country is composed. While I recounted the stories of past times to my young listeners, their features, their gestures, the forms of their language offered me, without their knowledge, another story, far deeper and more true. In some I recognized the ingenious races of the South, the Roman and Iberian blood of Provence and Languedoc, by which France binds herself to

Italy and Spain and which shall one day unite under its influence all the peoples of the Latin languages. In others I found the tough Celtic race, the resistant element of the ancient world, those hard heads with their enduring poetry and their insular nationality even on the continent. Elsewhere I recognized the conquering, quarrelsome people of Normandy, the most heroic of heroic times, the most industrious of the industrial era. Some, in their feeling for history, denoted good strong Flanders, land of fine deeds and fine lays, which gave Constantinople historians and emperors by turns. The blue eyes and blond heads of others made me think hopefully of that French Germany thrown like a bridge between two civilizations and two races. Finally, the absence of an indigenous character, imprecise features, a quick grasp, and a universal capacity announced Paris, the mind and the intellect of France.

Page 50. **Swift sword**... This is Gernot of the Nibelungen. Wherever sword thrusts are to be given or received, I wager there is a Frenchman present. At the battle of Nicopolis the captured crusaders found in the circle of Bajazet a Picard who had served Tamerlane before joining the Turks. The general of the armies of Cochin China today is one of our countrymen. The Frenchman is that naughty child that the mother of Duguesclin characterized: the one who always hits the others. In the history of our popular movements an essential element found only in France has been forgotten: the *gamin*. Let this careless, fearless child grow up; if he hasn't worn himself out prematurely, the little rascal can save the fatherland. In a military era, the *gamin*, formed, disciplined, tempered like steel by fatigue and by action in every climate, ultimately became that terrible guardsman, Bonaparte's *grognard*, presuming to judge his commander and following him always. In these two types, the *gamin* and the *grognard*, reside all the military genius of France.

Page 51. **The legislative people of modern times**... The science of law has two countries of origin, Rome and France, two eras, the second century and the seventeenth, and two authorities, Papinianus and Cujas. In the days of Cujas, the Germans doffed their hats at the mention of his name (see the *Life* by Berryat Saint-Prix). In our own time, also among the Germans, the *historical school* has restored the altars of Cujas. From the thirteenth century, France, with Italy, was regarded as the land of the law. An ancient German poet, having traveled through all the infidel *Welsch* lands, specifies the singularities of each: "I did not want to study magic under the necromancers of Dol, but I'll tell you how many lawyers there are in Vienne in the Dauphiné" (*Tanhuser*, cited by Goerres, *Altteutsche Volks- und Meisterlieder, aus den Handschriften. der Heidelberger Bibliothek*, 1817).

Page 52. **One should see what-all** *our men* **do in the ancient chronicles...** See, for example, *L'Histoire de Jean de Paris, roi de France*, printed at Troyes, and many other popular books. This is probably the most shameless bit of boasting put forward by any people.

Page 52. **The literature of France is eloquence and rhetoric... the people of rhetors and of prose writers...** All this is generally true. France lacks a poetry of images, but I am far from denying her a poetry of movement, which is also eloquence.

I cannot abandon this subject without observing how struck the ancients were by the rhetorical instinct and noisiness of the Gauls. *Nata in vanos tumultus gens* (Livy on the taking of Rome). Public criers, trumpeters, advocates were often Gauls. *Insuber, id est, Mercator et praeco* (Cicero, *In Pisonem*). See also the entire oration *Pro Fonteio*. "Pleraque Gallia duas res industriosissime persequitur, virtutem bellicam et argute loqui" (Cato, *In Charisio*? I cite from memory). Ἀπειληταὶ, καὶ ἀνατατικοὶ, καὶ τετραγῳδημένοι. (Diod. Sic., lib. IV.)

In the political assemblies of the Gauls, the orators often refused to yield the floor. Whereupon an usher, having twice demanded silence, approached the recalcitrant one, sword in hand, and cut off a panel of his cloak, enough to make the rest useless. Ὅσον ἄχρηστον ποιῆσαι τὸ λοιπόν. (Strab., VI, p. 197.)

The *Rederiker* or rhetoricians of the Low Countries were imitating France, not Germany (Grimm, *Über den Meistergesang*). By this very term Belgium avowed what France believed but had not understood: that literature is rhetoric. In the chambers of the rhetoricians, the poet was made to kneel and was obliged to reach the end of his poetic work before he could stand up again. These ridiculous conditions, and the prodigiously complicated metrics of the troubadours, show that rhetoricians and poets alike were mainly preoccupied with the merits of difficulty overcome.

Page 53. **Louis le Débonnaire...** Charles the Bald wrote of his brothers: "If only they had brought me before the tribunal of the bishops, my natural judges." But for the Norman invasions, which obliged France to take on a military and feudal character, the rule by bishops would have gone on.

Page 53. **Priests and kings then contrive to create communes and to gather there an anti-feudal army...** "Tum communitas in Francia popularis statuta est a praesulibus, ut presbyteri comitarentur regi ad obsidionem vel pugnam, cum vexillis et parochianis omnibus" (Orderic Vital., p. 836, ed. Duchesne).

Page 53. **At the same time that the local privileges of the communes are collapsing, the Estates General are established...** Deputies of the third estate summoned to the assembly of barons in 1302. From 1320 to 1375, suppression of the communes of Laon, Soissons, Meulan, Tournai, Péronne, Neuville, Roye, etc.

PAGE 54. **As adversary to the head of feudalism, the Emperor, France elevates and stands by the pontiff of Rome**... In a harangue before the Diet assembled at Besançon in 1162, the archbishop of Cologne and chancellor of Frederick Barbarossa called the kings of France and of England *provincial kings* (Saxo Gramm., I, 14). Emperor Henry VI wanted to require an oath of fidelity of the king of France (Innoc. III, ep. 64). In the cloisters of Germany the monks produced a play where all the kings of the world submitted to the emperor; the king of France resisted, aided by the antichrist (*Thesaur. Anecdot.*, II, pt. III, p. 187).

PAGE 54. **Confiscate the pontificate**... See above, in one of the notes on Italy, what tyranny Philip the Fair and Philip of Valois exercised over the popes during their time in Avignon. The house of France, which disposed over the authority of the Holy See, possessed the kingdom of Naples, and claimed that of Aragon, attracted the hatred and the jealousy of all Europe. Edward I and Edward III were regarded as the avengers of Christianity. One can gauge the animosity of the Italians by the famous passage in which Dante lets Hugues Capet speak. The poet takes the blind violence of his invective to the point of letting the founder of the third race be told that he is the son of a butcher of Paris:

> Io fui radice della mala pianta
> Che la terra Cristiana tutta aduggia,
> Si che buon frutto rado se ne schianta.
>
> Ma se Doaggio, Guanto, Lilla et Bruggia
> Potesser, tosto ne saria vendetta:
> Ed io la cheggio a lui che tutto giuggia.
>
> Chiamato fui di là Ugo Ciapetta:
> Di me son nati i Filippi, et i Luigi,
> Per cui novellamente è Francia retta:
>
> Figliuol fui d'un beccajo di Parigi,
> Quando li regi antichi venner meno
> Tutti, fuor ch'un renduto in panni bigi.
>
> Trovami stretto nelle mani il freno
> Del governo del regno e tanta possa
> Di nuovo acquisto, e più d'amici pieno,

Ch'alla corona vedova promossa
La testa di mio figlio fu, dal quale
Cominciar di costor le sacrate ossa.

Mentre che la gran dote Provenzale
Al sangue mio non tolse la vergogna,
Poco valea, ma pur non facea male.

Lì cominciò con forza et con menzogna
La sua rapina; et poscia per ammenda
Ponti et Normandi prese e Guascogna.

Carlo venne in Italia e per ammenda
Vittima fe' di Corradino, e poi
Ripinse al ciel Tommaso per ammenda.

Tempo vegg'io non molto dopo ancoi,
Che tragge un altro Carlo fuor di Francia
Per far conoscer meglio e se e I suoi.

Senz'arme n'esce, e solo con la lancia
Con la qual giostrò Giuda, e quella ponta,
Si, ch'a Fiorenza fa scoppiar la pancia.

Quindi non terra, ma peccato e onta
Guadagnerà per se, tanto più grave
Quanto più lieve simil danno conta.

L'altro che ci già usù, presso di nave.
Veggio vender sua figlia e patteggiarne,
Come fan li Corsar dell' altre schiave.

O avarizia, che puoi tu più farne,
Poi c'hai il sangue mio a te si tratto,
Che non si cura della propria carne?

Perchè men paja il mal futuro, e'l fatto.
Veggio in Alagna entrar lo fiordaliso,
E nel vicario suo Cristo esser catto.

Veggiolo un altra volta esser deriso:
Veggio rinnovellar l'aceto e'l fele,
E tra vivi ladroni essere anciso.

Veggio'l nuova Pilato si crudele,
One cio nol sazia, ma senza decreto
Porta nel tempio le cupide vele.

O signor mio, quando sarò io lieto,
A veder la vendetta, que nascosa
Fa dolce l'ira tua nel tuo segreto?

Dante, *Purgatorio*, XX

PAGE 54. **A saying in Provence in the twelfth century**... See Sismondi, *Littératures du midi de l'Europe*.

PAGE 54. **The king of France is presented as a citizen king.** Fleury says: "In France all private persons are free [he means, no doubt, in comparison with the rest of Europe]; there is no slavery; there is liberty of domicile, travel, commerce, marriage, choice of profession, acquisition and disposition of property, inheritance." In a curious passage Machiavelli makes the same judgment: "There have been many kings and very few good kings. I mean among absolute sovereigns, among whom one may not count the kings of Egypt of the most remote times, when that land was governed by laws; nor those of Sparta; *nor those of France* in modern times, where the government of the kingdom is the most tempered by law that we know of" (*Disc. Sopr. Tit. Liv.*, I, c. 8). Elsewhere he says: "The kingdom of France is content and peaceful because the king is subject to any number of laws that protect the peoples. *The one who set up that government* wanted kings to dispose freely over arms and the treasury; but for other matters, he put them under the rule of law" (*Disc.*, I, 16). Commines (V, ch. 19): "Is there king or baron on earth who has power except in his own demesnes to impose any levy on his subjects without the authorization and consent of those who are to pay it, unless it be by tyranny and violence? ... Our king is the lord who has least occasion to use the formula: *I have privilege of imposing what I please on my subjects*. For neither he nor another has such privilege; and they do him no honor who say he does, to make him seem more grand."

Page 54. **To disobey on pain of disobedience**... This order, given parliament by Louis XII, has been renewed more than once on other terms. It is not at all contradictory. In a prince there are two persons: the king and the man. The former forbade obedience to the latter.

Page 55. **England explains France, but by opposition**... See, in *L'Histoire de la Guerre de la Péninsule*, vol. I, by General Foy, an admirable tableau of the contrasts between the French and the English armies.

Page 55. **Human pride made flesh... obstacle to the fusion of the races and to the convergence of social station, , , the** *Satanic school*... The truest formula concerning an extremely complex subject must ignore numerous exceptions; precisely because it ignores exceptions, it is a formula and a true formula. England, to be sure, is trying to emerge from the state I have described, but the difficulty she has doing so proves my assertions. Consideration of the Reform Bill was ratified by a majority of *one vote*. In matters of religion, I see that England is making unbelievable efforts to believe. The ones fasten upon the letter, upon the Bible; the others let themselves be guided by the spirit—across wilderness and precipice. Nations themselves are often deceived about the state of their religious faith. For a certainty, the century of Louis XIV believed that it believed; Bossuet triumphed from the chancel. But behind triumphant Bossuet, somber Pascal was murmuring, and he alone had the pulse of the times, with a steady view into the abyss between Montaigne and Voltaire. As to England, her turn of mind is determined by her unvarying predilection for the three poets I have named. Her poetry is in three acts: *doubt, evil, and despair*. Shakespeare stands at the beginning of this terrible trilogy. As soon as England comes to herself again after the French wars, the Wars of the Roses, and the Reformation, her first cry is a bitter irony upon this world. Shakespeare mirrors the universe—minus God. Situated in the extreme west, England has felt the breath of the East less than any other people. Her literature is the most western, the most *heroic*, which is to say, the most dedicated to the pride of *self*. Western development reached its furthest point in Fichte, Byron, and the French Revolution. The moment of correction is about to arrive. The Germanic race, having come from India, has already returned there aboard the ships of England. Bonaparte, so French, so Italian, nonetheless already sympathizes with the East, above all with Muslim radicalism. Fatality pushed humanity from the East into the West; today we are returning voluntarily toward the East. English India will do for Asia what ancient India did for Europe.

Page 55. **The unbridled life of coursing and adventure... rulers of the sea, of a world without law and without limit**... Possession of the barren element (ἀτρυγέτοιο θαλάσσης) always produced that fierce pride. It explodes in Aeschylus. But in the Greek city the individual was too constrained to be able to reach full development. In addition, the Greek navy was extremely timid; those who never lost sight of the shore, who saw a fine temple atop every promontory were always well guided by the gods. On the boundless, solitary Ocean, by contrast... The *Corsair* of Byron and the first volume of Thierry (*Conquête de l'Angleterre, etc.*) are the true commentary on all this.

Page 55. **Egoism**... Sometimes egoism is a product of greed for pleasure, sometimes of the pride that disdains pleasure. Hence the prosaic tendencies of English industrialism alongside such sublime poetry. This explains how gentle Tuscany and industrial Florence could have bred Michelangelo, whose inspiration seems to have come from rage and disdain.

Page 55. **Evil, be thou my good**...

> Evil, be thou my good!...
> Down to bottomless perdition...

Milton, *Paradise Lost*, IV, 5, line 110; I, 5, line 17

Page 55. **The Gaul sings of the fast approaching humiliation of England**... See Thierry, *Conquête de l'Angleterre*, IV.

Page 56. **The iconoclastic warrior aristocracies of Persia and of Rome**... Plutarch (*Life of Numa*) tells us that the Romans did not worship images in the early centuries. I have pointed to certain other analogies between Persia and Rome elsewhere.

Page 56. *The one who always says, No*... See the speech of the shah (?) ... in Saint-Martin, *Histoire d'Arménie*.

Page 57. **Commonplace, prosaic...** *my name is legion.* Those who find this observation a bit harsh might recall that it is considered unforgivably ridiculous to be what we call *original* in matters of language and custom.

Page 57. **How the unmixed races eagerly drink up corruption**... To cite only one example, consider how our Merovingians bastardize themselves in short order. They reach the point where the last of them almost all die at age twenty.

Page 58. **And may this word be heard in Italy!** It may have been heard too well. Unhappy Bologna, in what condition will this book find you when it crosses the

Alps? Alas! A French city at heart! Which Dante longed to see supreme in language and spirit in Italy!

PAGE 59. **The child must quit its mother...** Here the somber and discouraging picture that the Ossian of German philosophy paints of this solemn moment:

"After the art of painting had cast its last ray of light, after Shakespeare had closed the gates of heaven, came a long sleep of death. The Antichrist was born... Earth had hung upon heaven as a nursling hangs upon its mother's breast; it was time for her, having become strong, to separate; the Reformation undertook to wean her. Today the earth spirit sorts through entrails of gold and of iron, searching for the bezoar that will heal it; the pallor of death marks its face; its bones ache; how could it think of the songs and the sounds of the lyre?... It is touching to see that the poets will not relent; the leaves have all turned yellow; each gust of wind strews the ground with them, and the child of poetry, not budging from its bough, still sings its sorrows, its hopes; the sun sinks further and further, the nights become longer and longer, the cold, dark powers dominate life more and more..."

PAGE 59. **Like Werner...** Or rather, Jean-Paul (Richter), I believe.

PAGE 60. **For nearly forty years...** It does seem that time has not been lost during this agitated period, not even for our well-being. In 1789 the average life span was 28 ¾ years; in 1831 it is 31 ½ years (*Annuaire du Bureau des Longitudes*, 1831).

PAGE 60. **Order will return...** Nowhere are there more landowners than here; nowhere are proletarians more free in their activity and therefore more able to cease to be proletarians; nowhere are the need and the instinct for centralization stronger. France is as if made to act upon the world and will enjoy central power longer than any other people; she, more than any other people, is a political person; action requires personality; personality does not exist without unity: a further guaranty of public order.

PAGE 60. *The Athenian said: Hail! City of Cecrops!...* I restore the entire passage here. It is perhaps the most beautiful of Marcus Aurelius:

Πᾶν μοι συναρμόζει ὃ σοὶ εὐάρμοστόν ἐστι, ὦ κόσμε· οὐδέν μοι πρόωρον, οὐδὲ ὄψιμον, τὸ σοὶ εὔκαιρον· πᾶν καρπὸς ὃ φέρουσιν αἱ σαὶ ὧραι, ὦ φύσις· ἐκ σοῦ πάντα, ἐν σοὶ πάντα, εἰς σὲ πάντα. Ἐκεῖνος μέν φησι, πόλι φίλη Κέκροπος· σὺ δὲ οὐκ ἐρεῖς, ὦ πόλι φίλη Διός.

O world, all that is in harmony with you is in harmony with me. For me nothing is too early, nothing too late that is in good time for you. O nature, whatever your seasons bring is fruitful. All things come from you, all things are in you, all things are for you. And the other said: "Beloved city of Cecrops." Do you then not say: "O beloved city of Jupiter!" (Lib. IV, 23.)

PAGE 61. **The Word of the social world**... The ancient world bequeathed to the modern as testament two expressions of admirable profundity: "Knowledge is the demonstration of faith" (Saint Clement of Alexandria) and "Man is liberty" (Proclus). It was the destiny of man to move by means of liberty from faith to knowledge. And knowledge itself is the most powerful means of liberty. Popularized knowledge is the means of an equal liberty, of a free equality, an ideal that humankind will approach more and more but never attain. With the result that another life is always necessary to complete the full development of man.

PAGE 63. **By placing ourselves on the summit of the Capitoline**... This is the lovely image of the elegant and ingenious author of *L'Histoire du Droit de succession*, which I have already cited (Gans, *Erbrecht*, vol. I).

PAGE 63. **The genius of Italy and of France**... **Rome is the crux of the drama**...This publication will be followed immediately by that of my history of Italy (*République Romaine*, pt. 1). May I therefore take the occasion to point out the unity of spirit that has presided in my work thus far and may I be forgiven for speaking, necessarily, of myself. In matters of method, questions proliferate; individuals matter little.

Having begun teaching early (since 1817) and without having enjoyed the advantage of courses at the École Normale, I was obliged to find my own way. For better or worse, my direction was my own. Obliged to teach successively, and often simultaneously, philosophy, history, and languages, I became aware of the intimate relationship, constantly before me, of the study of ideas and of facts, of the ideal and of the real. In the first enthusiasm that such a point of view could not fail to inspire in a young man, I conceived and prepared an *Essai sur l'histoire de la civilisation trouvée dans les langues*. But my serious and sustained work began only in 1824, in a treatment of *L'Unité des sciences qui font l'objet de l'enseignement classique* (printed but not published). In 1827 I produced simultaneously a piece on the philosophy of history and several essays on history or criticism (*Principes de la philosophie de l'histoire, traduits de la* Scienza nuova *de Vico; Précis de l'Histoire moderne; Vie de Zénobie* in *Biographie universelle*, etc.); I published similar work in 1831. The short philosophical essay that this note concludes will be followed by various more extensive historical studies. (*L'Histoire de la République romaine, Précis d'Histoire de France,* and the first two volumes of *L'Histoire de France* have appeared subsequently.)

No one will fail to see the connection between Vico's publication and the present one. In the philosophy of history, Vico has placed himself between Bossuet and Voltaire, both of whom he dominates. Bossuet had confined world history within a narrow frame and set an immutable limit to the development of humankind. Voltaire had denied this development and scattered history to the four winds by delivering it to blind chance. In the work of the Italian philosopher, the god of all ages and of all peoples shone for the first time over history: Providence. Vico is superior even to Herder. He understands humanity not as a plant that springs from the earth by organic development under the dew of heaven, but as the harmonic system of the civil world. To see man, Herder placed himself in nature; Vico places himself in man, in man making himself more human by means of society. This is what makes my good Vico the true prophet of the new order that is beginning and it is thus that his book deserves the name he dared to give it: *Scienza nuova.*

TRANSLATOR'S AND EDITOR'S NOTES

i   The reference is to *Voyages de monsieur le chevalier Chardin en Perse et autres lieux de l'Orient* (first edn., Amsterdam 1711). [Ed.]

ii   *Ayeen-Akbery: or The Institutes of the Emperor Akber*, translated by Francis Gladwin (Calcutta: William Mackay, 1774; London: G. Auld, 1800). [Ed.]

iii The play *Sakontala* or *Shakuntala* was translated from the Sanskrit into English by Sir William Jones and published in London in 1789 and again in 1807. It was known to Goethe and is the title of an opera by Franz Schubert. [Ed.]

iv   Joseph Guigniaut's translation of Georg Friedrich Creuzer's *Symbolik und Mythologie der Alten Völker* (1810-1812) was published in four volumes as *Religions de l'antiquité considérées principalement dans leurs formes symboliques et mythologiques* (Paris: Treuttel et Würtz, 1825-1841). [Ed.]

v   Michelet does not specify any one of many editions, from the seventeenth to the nineteenth century, of *Panegyrici veteres*. "Zozim." probably refers to Historiarum Herodianicas subsequentium libri II, or Herodiani Historiarum Romanorum libri VIII, ed. Henricus Stephanus Zozimus. [Ed.]

vi   Probably *Dei gesta per Francos* by Guibert de Nogent (eleventh—twelfth century). [Ed.]

vii *Historiarum libri quinque* by Rudolph Glaber (985-1047). [Ed.]

viii Michelet does not indicate clearly that—as pointed out by Aurélien Aramini in endnote ix below—this long note/clarification consists of a translation, freely adapted, from the German text in Brüder Grimm, *Altdeutsche Wälder*, vol. 1 (Cassel: Thurneissen, 1813) and vol. 3 (Frankfurt: Bernhard Körner, 1816). In addition, Michelet does not distinguish clearly between his translations of short passages from the Grimms' introduction (vol. 3, pp. 97-108) and his translations of the texts reproduced by the Grimms (vol. 3, pp. 109-148). Nor is the reader informed that the old texts about the hunter, given in a prose translation, are in rhyming verse in the original or that what is given in French translation is a selection, separated by large gaps, of verses that occupy over 40 pages in the original. Some verses have even been removed from their place in the original and resituated in the translation (e.g. "On your feet, cook and steward. Prepare a fine soup and a barrel of wine today, so that we can all live merrily"). The *Reception of a Companion Smith* and the *Reception of a Companion Cooper*, also much abbreviated (though omissions are here sometimes indicated by ellipses) are taken from vol. 1 of *Altdeutsche Wälder* (pp. 88-99 and pp. 100-122 respectively). On Michelet's free appropriation of his sources, see Stephen Bann, *The Clothing of Clio* (Cambridge: Cambridge University Press, 1984), pp. 33-35, 48. [Ed.]

ix   Original French: *les anciens joete, héros et nains, échangent des questions et se demandent des signes.* The word *joete* was not found in any dictionary of French or Old French, German (including Grimm), Dutch, Danish, Italian, Spanish, or Old Provençal. Nor is it the object of an explanatory note in any edition of the *Introduction à l'histoire universelle,* including that of Paul Viallaneix in volume 2 of his great 21-volume *Oeuvres complètes* (Paris: Flammarion, 1971-1987). An explanation of the term was solicited from Professor Paule Petitier, Professor of French Literature at the University of Paris Diderot-Paris 7, the author of many books and articles on Michelet and the co-editor, with Paul Viallaneix, of a multi-volume re-edition of Michelet's *Histoire de France* (Sainte-Marguerite sur Mer: Editions des Équateurs, 2006-2008). Several weeks after offering her own interpretation of the mysterious term, Professor Petitier communicated the following explanation of it, which had been sent to her by Aurélien Aramini, a doctoral candidate at the University of Besançon, and which she judged more convincing than her own. The editor and translator are grateful to both Professor Petitier and Aurélien Aramini for generously sharing the results of their research. Aurélien Aramini's note, freely translated by the editor and with some added references, follows [Ed.].

The term "joete" does not exist either in French or in German. For good reason. It was created by Michelet. Or, rather, he transcribed a German word into French. The long note in which the term appears is itself in large measure a translation—without quotation marks, as was often the practice of the philosopher-historian—of passages from *Altdeutsche Wälder,* vol. 3, by the brothers Jacob and Wilhelm Grimm (Frankfurt: Körner, 1816). The original German text runs as follows: "Wie die alten Jöten, Zwerge und Helden Rede wechseln und sich sichere Zeichen abfragen u.s.w." (p. 102).

Who are these "Jöten"? As the topic under discussion where the term appears is poetic symbolism, it probably refers to characters in Germanic mythology. There is no mention of "Jöten" or "Joete" in any French work of the Restoration period. On the other hand, the pagan pantheon of the Germanic tribes is described in several books in German. We know from an entry in his "Journal de mes lectures" [*Écrits de jeunesse: Journal (1820-1823), Mémorial, Journal des idées,* ed. P Viallaneix (Paris: Gallimard, 1959), p. 330] that in September 1828 Michelet read the *Wolsunga Saga* in [the first volume of] Friedrich von der Hagen's collection [of *Nordische Heldenromane uebersetzt durch Friedrich Heinrich von der Hagen* (Breslau: Josef Max und Kemp, 1815)]. He also translated passages from Jacob and Wilhelm Grimm in the notes to the *Introduction à l'histoire universelle.* There is no reason to believe that the philosopher-historian had not read or did not know of the German-language works on Germanic mythology that did exist. And "Jöten" are indeed part of Germanic mythology. In his *Mythologie der alten Teutschen und Slaven* (Znaim: Hofmann, 1827) Anton Tkany explains (p. 147) that the terms "Jetten, Jöten, or Jotun" refer "in Scandinavian mythology to giants who are also called Thussen and Krymthussen." Thus, like the "dwarves" or the "heroes," the "Jöten" are mythical figures, "perpetual enemies of the Ases (Gods)," according to Tkany, whose work, incidentally, was not unknown in France, since it is mentioned in the *Journal général de la littérature étrangère* in 1827. There is no doubt that Jacob and Wilhelm Grimm are referring to these mythical figures. Michelet's French version of the German "Jöten" as "joete" thus refers to those giants of Germanic and Scandinavian mythology.

x   *Ein Gespräch, die neun Gab-Musä oder Kunstgöttin betreffend* (1536). [Ed.]

xi   *Die Wittembirgisch Nachtigall die man yetz höret vberall.* [Ed.]

xii   "Mayer" probably refers to Johann Friedrich von Meyer (1772-1849), a German jurist and theosophist, author of a German translation of Cicero's *De natura deorum* (1806) and of a short volume *Zur Aegyptologie* (1840). "Kanne" is almost certainly Johann Arnold Kanne, author of *Pantheum der Aeltesten Naturphilosophie: Die Religion aller Völker* (1811). [Ed.]

xiii   Byron, *The Island*, II, xvii, 17-19. [Tr.]

xiv   Michelet quotes the first line of "Mignons Lied" from *Wilhelm Meisters Lehrjahre*, in "the elegant translation of M. Toussenel." [Tr.]

xv   Francesco Inghirami, *Monumenti etruschi o di etrusco nome* (Fiesole, 1821); Giuseppe Micali, *L'Italia avanti il dominio dei Romani* (Florence, 1810); Karl Otfried Müller, *Die Etrusker* (Breslau, 1828). [Ed.]

xvi   J.D. Fiorillo, *Geschichte der Künste und Wissenschaften* (Göttingen, 1798). [Ed.]

xvii   Wilelmus Goesius, *Rei agrariae auctores legesque variae* (Amsterdam, 1674). [Ed.]

4. Opening Address at the Faculty of Letters, 9 January 1834

Jules Michelet

Translated by Lionel Gossman[1]

1   This translation is based upon the following edition: J. Michelet, *Introduction à l'histoire universelle, suivi du Discours d'ouverture prononcé à la Faculté des Lettres le 9 janvier 1834* (Paris: Librairie Classique de L. Hachette, 1834). This edition is available at http://bit.ly/1a2aO45

DOI: 10.11647/OBP.0036.04

(Collége de France. — Salle des Cours.)

Fig. 3. 'Ouverture des Cours au Collège de France et à la Sorbonne',
L'Illustration, 46/2, 13 January 1844

Gentlemen:

To speak of history in such a profoundly historic place is a weighty matter. Overwhelmed by the view of these walls, which call up so many memories, and of this audience, gathered together from every part of France, I have difficulty finding words. At this single moment and in this confined space history appears before me in all its immensity and variety, in all the complexity of its times and places. As early as the thirteenth century, as early as the reign of Saint Louis, the name of Sorbonne stood for the great school of France, indeed of the world. The most illustrious men of the Middle Ages sat on these benches. The Hibernian subtlety of Duns Scotus, the passion for Africa of Raymond Lull, the poetic idealism of Petrarch—everything came together here. Those who could find no resting place—the author of the *Gerusalemme* and the author of the Divine Comedy, the "Florentine exile," the wandering observer of three worlds—stopped here for a moment. In the seventeenth century, this hall, rehabilitated by Richelieu, witnessed the first efforts of Malebranche, the Christian Plato, and the tough battles of Arnaud.[2] Fénelon, Molière, and Voltaire were raised only steps away. Pascal and Rousseau did much of their writing in the shadow of the exterior walls of the chapel, in an obscure little street nearby. In this very place, a student, M. Turgot, then a young man of twenty-five, presented a dissertation in which he laid the true foundations of the philosophy of history. France, Gentlemen, will never forget how brilliantly history—the history of philosophy, the history of literature, political history—was taught only recently from this very chair. Who will revive for me the day when I saw my illustrious predecessor and friend[3] step back up to the rostrum, when we heard him hold forth, for the

2 Antoine Arnaud (1612-1694) was a French Jansenist theologian and mathematician, known for his polemics against the Jesuits and the philosopher Malebranche. [Ed.]
3 François Guizot (1787-1874), eminent French liberal statesman and historian. On his appointment as Minister of Education under Louis-Philippe in October 1832 he was temporarily replaced by Michelet in the chair of modern history at the Sorbonne. The author

second time,[4] in those simple, strong, limpid and creative words, by which science was freed from every passing passion, from every partiality, from all falseness of fact or style, and history raised to the dignity of law.

From the most distant past to our own time, such, Gentlemen, has been the noble perdurance of the traditions attached to the place where we are now. This house of Sorbonne is old; it knows a lot, cleaned and touched up to look new as it may be. Centuries have lived in it and each one has left something of itself. Whether you perceive it or not, the trace is there, do not doubt it for a moment, just as in a human heart! People and houses, we all bear the imprint of ages past. As young men, we carry within us countless ideas and ancient feelings of whose presence we are unaware. These traces of times long past are jumbled inside us, indistinct, often disturbing. We turn out to know things we never learned, to have memories of things we never witnessed; and we feel the dull reverberations of the emotions of people we never knew. Surprise is expressed at the seriousness in the faces of the young. Our fathers ask why in this age of strength we proceed bent and pensive. It is because history is in us, we feel the weight of the centuries, we are the bearers of the world.

I would like, Gentlemen, to analyze with you those complex elements that are the more troublesome as they are barely distinguishable; I would like to grasp how much in what emerged only yesterday is very ancient; I would like to explain to myself, as a modern man, my own birth, to tell myself the story of the long trials I have endured over the last five centuries, and to explore the dark and painful passage by which, after so much weary struggling, I have come into the daylight of civilization and liberty.

This is a grave, solemn, and immensely difficult topic. We have to explain how, sunk in the obscure impersonality of the Middle Ages, man came gradually to reveal himself to himself, how the individual came to count for something in the world and to acquire an existence in his own name. A slave no more, no more a serf. The slave, from now on, is the world of matter, subdued and made into a servant by human industry. Antiquity debased man to the level of a thing; the modern age is elevating material nature, ennobling it through art, humanizing it. A more just society now rests on a foundation of equality. Civil order has

of many works of history, Guizot is best known for his *Histoire générale de la civilisation en Europe* (1828) and his 4-volume *Histoire de la civilisation en France* (1830). [Ed.]

4   Originally appointed to the chair of modern history in 1812, Guizot had been relieved of his functions in 1822, but was reinstated in 1828. Michelet presumably heard him lecture before 1822 and again "for the second time" in 1828. [Ed.]

been established, liberty has been won... And let anyone dare to take it away from us! ...

What a price our fathers paid to bring us to this point! No matter how hard history tries, we will never take the measure of it. So much struggle, so much bloodshed, so much destruction! The dramatic moments of combat and revolution have been recorded. But of the long centuries of suffering, the terrible misery of the people, the endless famines that ravaged it, the frightful torments it endured during the English wars, the wars of religion, the Hundred Years' War, the wars of Louis XIV—of all that very little has been said. We, the latecomers, have the benefit of it all. All the centuries have worked for us. The fourteenth and the fifteenth gave us our country. To give us freedom of religion, the sixteenth had to undergo fifty years of horrible little wars, skirmishes, ambushes, assassinations—war waged by dagger blows and pistol shots. The eighteenth waged its war with lightning bolts, and yet it created the society in which we still live. It was a sudden creation. To bring it about, fathers begrudged nothing; if something was needed, they opened their veins and gave their blood without restraint... Thus every age made its contribution, all of them suffered and struggled, without considering whether they themselves would benefit. They died without foresight of the future... We who know, Gentlemen, we who have harvested the fruits of their labour, let us bless them, and let us work so that we in turn will be blessed "by those who will refer to this time as *ancient times.*"

The year 1300 marks a solemn period in history. Boniface VIII proclaimed it his jubilee year, as if announcing by this pompous celebration the end of papal domination of Europe. Huge crowds gathered in Rome; pilgrims were counted by the hundreds of thousands until, soon, their numbers could no longer be counted and neither houses nor churches could accommodate them. They camped out in the streets and squares in hastily constructed shelters, under canvas, in tents, or under the canopy of heaven. It was as if at the end of time, the human race had appeared before its judge in the valley of Josaphat. Dante, the great poet of the Middle Ages, was then in Rome, and the spectacle was not lost on him. The Pope had summoned all the living to Rome. In his poem, the poet called upon all the dead; he reviewed the world that was gone, made order in it, and judged it. The Middle Ages appeared before him, as did Antiquity. Nothing remained hidden from him. The secret of the sanctuary was spoken and profaned. The seal was seized and broken; and it has not been found again since. The

Middle Ages had had its time of life, for life is a mystery and it is spent once the mystery has been fully revealed. The revelation of the Middle Ages was the *Divina Commedia*, Cologne Cathedral, the frescoes of the Campo Santo in Pisa. Thus art comes to end and close a civilization, to crown it and lay it in glory in its grave.

The life of the old world that died then had been sustained by two principles of order: the Holy Roman Pontificate and the Holy Roman Empire, two universal hierarchies, two orders, two absolutes, two infinites. Two infinites existing simultaneously are an absurdity. A dual order is disorder. How unstable in fact the two hierarchies were is well known. Still, this legal fiction simplified life to some extent. There was no question but that the baron was under the authority of the count, the count under that of the king, while the king himself did not fail to recognize the Emperor as the head of the feudal world. Everyone had his place and a predictable path that had been laid out in advance. One was born and one died according to a prescribed order. If life was sad and hard, at least death had a good pillow.

Indeed, when all that began to shake and the edifice in which one's place had been set for eternity started to totter, mankind was not at all inclined to rejoice. That development was not seen, as might have been expected, as a liberation. Instead, there was immense sadness. Everyone clasped his hands in prayer and said: "What is going to become of us?"

It was, Gentlemen, as though, with a hostile planet approaching ours, our laws suspended and the harmony of things upset, you were to see this building of ours wobble, the ground under us shift, the mountains move, and Mont Blanc topple and start heading toward the Pyrenees.

First, the two colossal figures of the time, the Pope and the Emperor, clashed in face-to-face conflict. The world formed a circle around the duelling pair. Strange things began to happen. The head of the Holy Roman Empire called in the Saracens to fight against Christians, and settled them in Italy, facing Rome; he shook hands with the Sultan; he wrote—at least according to tradition—the book of The Three Impostors, Moses, Mahomet, and Jesus Christ.[5] On the other side, the Pope, the priest, the man of peace, took up the sword, threw off the stole and turned his archbishop's cross into a club; he sold his keys and his mitre, he sold himself to France, in

---

5   The treatise *De tribus impostoribus* (c. 1230) denied all three Abrahamic religions— Judaism, Christianity, and Islam. It was attributed to a variety of authors. [Ed.]

order to kill the Emperor. He did kill him, but he himself died of it, leaving his goad and his life in the wound.

The laborious care with which, at this time, the two adversaries endeavour to demonstrate that they are alive is a grave sign of death. Never before have they shouted so loudly or made such grandiose claims. From the depths of their sepulchres, they flail about, they declaim, they gesticulate wildly. Their supporters proudly repeat crazy statements, which at the time inspired terror—acts of bravado in the face of death, the insolence of the void. On one side, Bartolus of Saxoferrato[6] announces that every soul owes obedience to the Emperor, that the spiritual world belongs to him no less than the temporal world, that he is "the living law." "Not so," retorts the Pope's defender, Brother AugustinusTriumphus.[7] "The Pope's authority is infinite, *immense*. By *immense* I mean immeasurable, by weight or by number. The Pope is more than a man, more than an angel, since he represents God on earth." And if Bartolus refuses to concede, the monks, provoked to the limit, will respond that "between the sun of the Papacy and the moon of the Empire there is this crucial difference, that the earth being seven times larger than the moon and the sun eight times larger than the earth, the Pope is exactly forty-seven times greater than the Emperor."

Whatever one may think of this strange arithmetic, whatever the degree of difference between the two competitors, both are by then very diminished. For that is the moment when one of them, by his Golden Bull, gives up the chief rights of the Empire.[8] In this final comic scene, the Electors respectfully relieve the Emperor of his power; they build him a table six feet high, they serve him at table, but on this table they have him sign his own demotion and their appropriation of power. The time is not far off when this master of the universe will have to use his horses as security to borrow from merchants no longer willing to give him credit and will flee for fear of being held captive by the butchers of the German city of Worms. A pathetic imperial dignity, dragging its prideful wretchedness along with it, will be a fugitive under Charles IV, a captive under Maximilian. The latter will serve the King of England for a hundred crowns a day until he manages to settle his affairs through a marriage and is kept going thanks to his wife.

6　Bartolus of Saxoferrato (1313-1357), a promiment Italian jurist and professor of law. [Ed.]

7　Augustinus Triumphus or Augustinus de Ancona (1243-1328), a monk noted for his advocacy of papal sovereignty, was the author of *Summa de potestate ecclesiastica* (completed in 1326). [Ed.]

8　The Golden Bull was issued in 1356 by the Imperial Diet under Emperor Charles IV. [Ed.]

The Pope, on his side, is neither less proud nor less humiliated. Slapped in the person of Boniface VIII by his good friend, the King of France, he places himself under the King's protection. In order to become Pope, as Clement V, the Gascon Bertrand de Got concludes a secret pact in the dark forest of Saint-Jean d'Angely: there, some say, he kisses the devil's claw; according to others it is the hand of Philippe-le-Bel that he kisses. In accordance with this Satanic deal, the Templars will perish and with them the memory of the Crusades; Boniface VIII's reputation will be stained; the Pope will declare that the Pope is fallible. In other words, the Papacy will destroy itself; the judge will condemn himself; the immovable will have retreated.

What is also harsh in the Pope's penitence is that he is forced by the King of France to continue damning the Emperor whom he no longer hates. "Alas," Benedict XII tells followers of the Emperor who come to him seeking absolution, "the King of France will not have it. He has already threatened to treat me worse than Boniface VIII." Philippe de Valois did indeed hold the Pope and the Papacy in the palm of his hand. Against the Papacy he had the support of his University, his Sorbonne. For a short time, he threatened John XXII with burning at the stake, as a heretic. "In matters of faith," he wrote to him, "we have people here who are far more knowledgeable than your legists in Avignon."

There you see, Gentlemen, how low the two great powers that in the Middle Ages represented law — the Holy Roman Empire and the Papacy — had sunk. Where will the idea of law, hitherto entrusted to these two representatives of the temporal and the spiritual power, find a new home? Man is now released from the age-old path; his pre-set track is vanishing before his eyes; he now has to see for himself and find his own direction. Thought, which until then had had support and was persuaded that it could not sustain itself on its own, finds that it has been left an orphan. Alone, timid and frail, it now has to find its own way in the vast empty spaces of the world.

It keeps on going, with the new guides who aim to lead it walking by its side. These guides — Franciscans and Dominicans — still speak in the name of the Church. They are monks, but itinerant monks, mendicant monks. They have none of the sombre austerity of the Middle Ages. Humanity has nothing to fear. They create a little flower-strewn path for it; if there is a messy patch, they throw down their cloaks for it to walk on. Nimble and facetious preachers, they lighten the boredom of the spiritual journey.

They have a repertoire of good stories, which they tell, sing, dramatise and enact. They have one for every rank and for every age. Faith, elastic in their hands, can be extended or shrunk at will. Everything has been made easy. After the Jewish law comes the Christian law; after Christ, Saint Francis. Saint Francis and the Virgin are quietly substituted for Jesus Christ. The boldest of them proclaim that the time of the Son is over; it is now the turn of the Holy Ghost. In this way Christianity serves as a form and vehicle for an anti-Christian philosophy. Authority is brought down by those it had designated to defend it.

While the monks lure the people into their roving mysticism, the jurists, immobile in their seats, are no less energetic in promoting movement. It might seem at first that these jurists, the damned souls of kings and the founders of monarchical despotism, cannot be counted among the liberators of thought. Enveloped in their robes of ermine, they speak only in the name of authority; they resuscitate the legal procedures of the Empire, as well as torture and secret sentencing. They summon the human spirit to walk straight, along the path laid out by Roman law. In the Pandects, they show it the road it has to follow. No more, no less. This is *reason in writing*. If humanity ventures to ask for something else, they do not hear, they do not understand, they shake their heads: *Nihil hoc ad edictum praetoris.*[9] These men have lived all through the Middle Ages without taking any notice of them. The date, for them, has remained unchanged since Tribonian. They are the Seven Sleepers who lay down under Justinian and woke up in the eleventh century. When the pontifical and feudal world invokes the authority of time, the jurists smile, they ask "how old?"; that young antiquity of a few centuries seem pitiful to them. Rome is their religion too, but it is the Rome of Roman Law. And that Rome emboldens them in their opposition to the other one. It is one of their number who goes forth and coolly *apprehends* the successor of the Apostles. Politely, in the name of the "liberties of the Galllican Church," they carry on this struggle, begun by a slap, for five hundred years. Applying their Roman law of succession, which requires that fiefs be divided up, they quietly dismantle the feudal system. They restore the monarchical regime of Justinian. With great learning they prove to kings that the king possesses all rights; they reduce everything to a single level under one master.

---

9   "This has nothing to do with the Praetor's Edict." On the Praetor's Edict, a central element in Roman Law, see the Wikipedia article http://en.wikipedia.org/wiki/Praetor's_Edict or the article "Praetor" in Encyclopedia Britannica. [Ed.]

In their demolition of the pontifical and feudal world, the jurists proceed methodically. They first defend the Emperor against the Pope; then they push the king of France into opposing the Pope and the Emperor. It is certainly no fault of theirs if the feudal world is not decapitated in the person of the latter. That world is crumbling. When France rises on the ruins of the Empire, which had claimed sovereignty over her; when the king of France, transformed from the representative of God into that of the devil, from Saint Louis into Philippe-le-Bel, begins under the guidance of the jurists to claim universal sovereignty, his vassal, the king of England responds on behalf of all with a brutal *No*; more yet, he has the impertinence to unseat his lord. "I," he says, "am king of France."

A furious war breaks out. It begins as a war between two kings and continues as a war between two peoples. England, small but strong, comes to shake up a sleeping France. After the long enchantment of the Middle Ages it is a deep sleep. In order to reach the people, the English must pass by way of the nobility. The latter, beaten at Crécy, captured and held to ransom at Poitiers, shuts itself up in its castles. The English cannot draw it out of them. The most outrageous provocations are barely enough. Five or six times the nobility refuses battle with armies double and triple in size. The English then turn against the man of the people, the peasant. His trees and his vines are cut down, he is starved and beaten, his house is set on fire, his pig slaughtered, his wife seized, his future harvest becomes fodder for their horses... So much is done to him that *Jacques le bonhomme* wakes from his sleep, opens his eyes, feels his muscles, moves his arms. Made furious by his misery and having nothing to lose, he hurls himself at his lord, who has defended him so poorly, and breaks his clogs on his lord's head. This is referred to as the *Jacquerie*. Jacques has discovered his strength. When the foreigners come back, he also has a sense of his rights. He gets the idea that God is on the side of the French. Even the women then become involved; they set aside their distaff and lead their men-folk to the enemy. This time Jacques' name is *Jeanne*; *Jeanne la Pucelle*, Joan of Arc.

France is much indebted to the English. It is England that teaches her to know herself. England is her pitiless guide in this painful initiation, the demon that tempts and tests her, that pricking her in the loins with its goad, pushes her round those circles of Dante's Inferno—which we call the history of the fourteenth century. Those were hard times, Gentlemen. First a horrendous war between peoples, and, simultaneously, another war, the fiscal war between government and people, with the nascent government administration living from day to day on confiscations, counterfeit money, and bankruptcies, and the exchequer extorting from the starving population what was needed to pay the soldiers that were plundering it. Gold once again became, as in the heyday of Carthage, the god of the world, and in the condottieri of all nations the abominable impiousness of the ancient mercenaries was revived.

Here and there the historians let fall a few words that give us a glimpse of a vast world of suffering. "At this time," according to one of them, "from Laon to Germany, not a building outside of the fortified places was left standing." "In the year 1348," Froissart tells us casually, "there was a sickness, called an epidemic, from which a third of the population of the world died."

Everything, indeed, seemed to be dying. The high inspiration of the great poems of chivalry was followed by the obscene mockery of the fabliaux. The world had no taste for anything but the licentious writings of Boccaccio. Poetry seemed to have been displaced by the short tale and by history; the ideal by reality. Between Joinville and Froissart Villani appears, cold and judicious.[10]

This general triumph of prose over poetry—which, after all, was simply the intimation of a step forward in progress toward maturity, toward the virile age of the human race—was taken as a sign of death. As happened just before the year 1000, everyone imagined that the end of the world was imminent. Some went so far as to predict the exact time when this would happen. First it was to be in the year 1260; then a delay was obtained until 1303, then again until 1335. In 1360, however, the world was certain of its end. There would be no remission.

But nothing was coming to an end. Everything kept going on. Nevertheless, everything seemed to become shadowy and shrouded in darkness. People became frightened; they did not know that they were going through night towards a new day. Whence those vague expressions of a sadness that was always incomprehensible to itself; whence the dull sufferings of Petrarch and those endless tears that he watches, simple-mindedly, dropping into the fountain at Vaucluse. But it falls to the author of the *Divine Comedy* to gather up all the unease and turmoil that is felt at that time. Abandoned by the old world while the other one is not yet

---

10 Giovanni Villani (c. 1276-1348), Florentine banker, official and diplomat, and author of the *Nuova Cronica*. See the article in the *Catholic Encyclopedia* http://www.newadvent.org/cathen/15429b.htm [Ed.]

visible, making his descent into the pit of Hell and barely distinguishing the faint glimmerings of Purgatory, dangling between a vanishing Virgil and a Beatrice who has not appeared, he has the impression that everything he is leaving behind has been turned upside down, the wrong way round. The infernal pyramid seems to him to be standing on its apex. Yet through that apex the two worlds come into contact, the world of darkness and the world of daylight. One more effort, and light will return. Having made this difficult crossing, the poet can now cry out "Sweet hue of eastern sapphire, that was spread o'er the serene aspect of the pure air, high up as the first circle."[11]

Gentlemen, you must never despair. In our time, as in Dante's, you will often hear sad and discouraging words. You will be told that the world is old, that it is fading away with each passing day, that down here the divine idea is being eclipsed. Do not believe a word of it. As for me, if I thought that it was so I would never have undertaken to tell you this sad story, I would never have accepted this chair. No, Gentlemen, in the midst of ever changing forms something immutable subsists. This world that we inhabit is still the city of God. The polity we created at such high cost is divine in justice and morality. The power of sacrifice has not been abolished. Our century is not more destitute of dedicated souls than any other. The eternal law has its devotees who will follow it unto death. In our own day we have known such dedicated individuals, whose pure lives were crowned by an heroic death. We did not know those who in ages long past gave their lives for their faith. But we too have seen and touched martyrs. Their relics are neither in Rome nor in Jerusalem; they are in our midst, in our streets, in our public squares; every day we remove our hats as we pass their tombs.

Whatever doubts and uncertainties we may have in times of transition, let us have faith in progress, in science, in liberty. Let us tread boldly over this earth; it will not fail us. The hand of God does not fail itself. We are still—you must believe this—in the embrace of Providence and, as has been noted in the case of the solar system, Providence has placed in this world a curative and reparative power that compensates for seeming irregularities. What we often take to be a breakdown is in reality a necessary passage, a periodic crisis that is not without precedents and that returns in due course.

---

11 Dolce color di oriental zaffiro/ che s'accoglieva nel sereno aspetto/ del mezzo, puro infino al primo giro (Dante, *Purgatorio*, I, lines 13-15). [Ed., with thanks to the eminent Dante scholar, Robert Hollander, for locating this passage.]

It is to history that we must turn, it is facts that we must investigate when the idea falters and drifts away before our eyes. Let us look to centuries past; let us spell out and interpret those prophecies of old. It may be that we will discover in them an early ray of light coming from the future. Herodotus tells us that some Asian people or other having promised the crown to whoever would be the first to see the dawn of day, everyone looked to the East; one individual only, more shrewd than the others, turned to look in the opposite direction and indeed, while the Orient was still shrouded in darkness, perceived in the West the first glimmer of dawn already shedding a white light on the top of a tower.

5. Preface to the History of France (1869)

Jules Michelet

Translated by Edward K. Kaplan[1]

---

1   This translation, now revised, was originally prepared for my book, *Michelet's Poetic Vision: A Romantic Philosophy of Nature, Man, and Woman* (Amherst: University of Massachusetts Press, 1977), with the assistance of Perry Mcintosh. The edition used was that of Charles Morazé (Paris: Armand Colin, 1962), and checked against Michelet's *Oeuvres complètes*, volume IV, ed. Paul Viallaneix (Paris: Flammarion, 1974). An edition by Gabriel Monod is available to read on-line at http://www.gutenberg.org/ebooks/38243

DOI: 10.11647/OBP.0036.05

Fig. 4. Jules Michelet, Histoire de France (Paris: Hetzel, 1869), 5 vols.,
vol. 1. frontispiece. Library of the Institute for Advanced Study, Princeton, New Jersey.

Introduction

Edward K. Kaplan

Jules Michelet faced impending death, and the completion of his life's work, with a sweeping Preface to the 1869 edition of his *History of France*. (The final volume had gone to press in October 1867.) This Romantic declaration of faith, shadowed by the crumbling Second Empire, and barely preceding the disasters of Sedan and the Commune, bears witness to the fervent vision of universal freedom which sustained the historian during his "arduous labor of almost forty years."

Moved by his persistent need for self-examination—and self-justification—Michelet's Preface to his completed *History* continues the autobiographical "Letter to Edgar Quinet" that introduces *The People* (1846), as Michelet surveys his vast ambitions while asserting how they were fulfilled.

Michelet firmly asserts his uniqueness among other historians. He distinguishes himself from his most illustrious French predecessor, Augustin Thierry (1795-1856), whose *Histoire de la Conquête de l'Angleterre par les Normands* (The Norman Conquest of England) appeared in 1825. Michelet's preoccupation with Thierry is perhaps due to the fact that their conceptions of historical writing—boldly original at the time—were strikingly similar. The narratives of both were admired for their lively style. Both attempted to reconcile art and science; and both were among the first to use original sources—such as manuscripts—to correct contemporary chronicles upon which most historical writing was then based. At the very least, Michelet is right to argue that he improved upon his elder's excessive focus on the element of race.

Michelet proudly proclaimed himself to be the first to perceive France "as a person and as a soul." As he had written a quarter of a century earlier in *The People*: "Thierry called history narration, and Guizot called it analysis. I have named it resurrection, and this name will last."[2]

Michelet celebrates the decisive influence on his vocation of the Neapolitan philosopher Giambattista Vico (1668-1744). In 1827 he was the first to introduce Vico's thought to the French public by his translation of Vico's *Scienza nuova*, and he remained Vico's enthusiastic disciple for his entire life.

However, Michelet fails to mention another decisive model (also influenced by Vico), the German philosopher of history, Johann Gottfried von Herder (1744-1803). In fact Herder's *Ideen* was translated and published the same year by Michelet's closest friend, Edgar Quinet (1803-1875). For Michelet, Herder is Vico's invisible partner.

Two themes dominate Michelet's professional and spiritual manifesto: the artistic problem of historical recreation and Michelet's changing attitude toward the Roman Catholic Church.

As an "artist-historian," Michelet repeatedly asserts his ambition to resurrect the integral life of the past. Armed with imaginative empathy, his task resembles the descent of Aeneas into the underworld. Like the historian, the Roman carried a golden bough which allowed him to enter and return unharmed from the realm of the dead. Michelet's golden bough was his self-knowledge as a writer with the imaginative power to revive the silenced voices he studies.

Resurrection of the past was an essentially prophetic task, a vision of universal justice. The dead would receive their reward of eternity by surviving in the consciousness of the present. The historian's sacred duty was to restore the glories of the past to inspire readers to construct the image of an ideal future.

In *The People* Michelet illustrates this grandiose aspiration as "Caesar's dream," an imperial image of the historian's vocation:

---

2   *The People,* translated by John P. McKay (Urbana: University of Illinois Press, 1973), p. 19. The next quotation from *The People* is from p. 152.

It is said that when Caesar was coasting along the shores of Africa, he fell asleep and had a dream; he saw a vast army, weeping and stretching their hands toward him. After awakening, he wrote upon his tablets "Corinth" and "Carthage," and he rebuilt those cities.

I am not Caesar, but how often have I dreamed Caesar's dream! I saw them weeping, I understood their tears. "*Urbem orant.*" They want their city! And I, a poor solitary dreamer, what could I give to that great silent nation? All that I had—my voice. May it be their first admission into the City of Right, from which they have been excluded until now!

The historian is a Promethean titan who initiates a rebirth of civilizations.

Michelet had only one serious competitor—the Roman Catholic Church. Their common goal was to define humanity and to decipher the meaning of universal history. Michelet's religious evolution reflects that of his nation, from medieval feudalism to the 1789 Revolution. His devotion to human freedom could not tolerate the Church's reactionary politics or theology of passive grace. He thus rejected his spiritual mother while remaining fitfully ambivalent toward her noble ideals.

As part of the generation that reached maturity during the Restoration, Michelet was nourished by his sympathy for the medieval Church. The six volumes of his *History of the Middle Ages* pulse with admiration for the artistic and intellectual triumphs of the Christian spirit. Because of the fervor expressed in these volumes, and because of the exhaustive documentation upon which they are based, most historians agree that they are Michelet's most lasting historical masterpiece. Does their literary quality suffice to explain why the author of the 1869 *Preface*, despite his long-standing hostility toward the Church, persisted in recalling his youthful love?

Political and personal circumstances had turned the historian into a rabid anticlerical. By 1843, the year of his public lessons attacking the Jesuits, his break with the Church was definitive. Yet, curiously, the *Preface* defends his youthful appreciation of the religion.

His defensive fidelity to his volumes of medieval history can be explained in part by his fundamental attraction to all sorts of spirituality, be they natural, human, or even supernatural. Perhaps a clearer explanation of his compulsion to recall his love of Christianity is his absolute commitment to an organic conception of historical writing. For the author, esthetic integrity became more compelling than ideology or the rectification of details.

Michelet's foremost goal was to depict the enduring legend of the French people, starting with its appearance as the peasant Jacques, through Joan of

Arc, and culminating in the French Revolution. The principle that *"humanity is its own Prometheus"* (derived from Vico) outweighs any discontinuity his own avowed changes of political opinion might betray. Michelet's mission remained constant from the quasi-mystical illumination brought about by the July Revolution to his death in 1874: liberate human energy, celebrate the inherent powers of nature.

Michelet draws his most intimate self-portrait as he evokes the creator's love for his subjects. Writing, for the Romantic historian, resembles a woman's gestation of a child. Michelet indeed possessed what he called the "two sexes of the mind," the historian's unique combination of "male" analysis and "female" compassion and empathy. He had absorbed ten centuries of struggle, "swallowed too many plagues, too many vipers, and too many kings." He loved or detested his actors with deep passion.

Jules Michelet, the person and the writer, lives still in these pages. His work recapitulates an entire nation and exemplifies the sublimity, and the frailty, of a great and tender heart.

Preface to the History of France (1869)

Jules Michelet

This arduous labor of about forty years was conceived in an instant, in the lightning flash of the July Revolution. During those memorable days a great light appeared, and I perceived France.

She possessed annals, but no history at all. Eminent men had studied her, especially from the political point of view. None of them entered into the infinite details of the diverse products of her activity (religious, economic, artistic, etc.). None of them had yet embraced the living unity of the innate and geographic elements which formed her. I was the first to perceive her as a soul and as a person.

The renowned Sismondi, a persevering worker, honest and discerning, rarely elevates himself to comprehensive views in his political annals. Moreover, he scarcely undertakes scholarly research. He himself dutifully admits that, writing in Geneva, he had neither the records nor the manuscripts at hand.

Besides, until 1830 (even until 1836), none of the remarkable historians of that period had yet felt the need to seek facts outside of printed books, from original sources—for the most part unpublished at the time—and from the manuscripts in our libraries, from documents in our archives.

That noble historical constellation which, from 1820 to 1830, caused so great a stir—MM. de Barante, Guizot, Mignet, Thiers, AugustinThierry—considered history from specialized and differing points of view. One was preoccupied with the racial element, another with institutions, etc., perhaps not understanding adequately how difficult it is to isolate these things, how each of them works upon the others. Do races, for example, remain the same without being influenced by changing customs? Can institutions be sufficiently studied without taking into account the history of ideas and the multitude of social conditions from which they arise? There is always something artificial about these specializations, which claim to illuminate, but which nonetheless might give faulty profiles, deceiving us about the whole, concealing the greater harmony.

Life has one supreme and very exacting condition. It is genuinely life only when complete. All its organs are interdependent and work only as a whole. Our vital functions are linked, presuppose one another. If one is missing, nothing will live any longer. In the past it was believed possible to isolate by the scalpel, to follow separately each of our systems; this cannot be, for everything influences everything.

Thus, either all or nothing. To rediscover historical life, one must follow it patiently along its paths, in all its forms, all its components. But one must also, with a still greater passion, reconstruct and restore all its workings, the reciprocal action of these diverse forces in a powerful motion which would again become life itself.

Géricault, a master with whom I shared, not genius no doubt, but a violent will, upon entering the Louvre (the Louvre of that time, where all Europe's art was collected), did not seem troubled. He said: "Fine! I'll do it all over again." In rapid sketches which he never signed, he went about seizing and appropriating everything. And, were it not for 1815, he would have kept his word. Such are the passions, the madness of youth.

Still more complicated, more terrifying, was the problem I had set for myself as an historian: the *resurrection of life in its integrity,* not superficially, but in its interior and organic depth. No prudent man would have dreamed of it. Fortunately, that I was not.

In the blazing dawn of the July Revolution, in its vast hope, its powerful electricity, this superhuman undertaking did not frighten a young heart. At certain times there are no obstacles. Everything is simplified by the flame. In it a thousand confused things are clarified, rediscover their true connections, and (harmonizing themselves) are illuminated by each other. Many springs, inert and heavy when they lie apart, begin acting of their own accord if they are placed back into the whole.

Such was my faith at least, and that act of faith, whatever my weaknesses, took effect. History's immense movement started to heave before my eyes. All those various forces, both of nature and of art, sought each other out, took their places, at first awkwardly. The limbs of the great body, peoples, races, regions, assembled themselves from the sea to the Rhine, to the Rhône, to the Alps, and the centuries marched from Gaul to France.

Everyone, friends and enemies, said "that it was alive." But what are the true, unquestionable signs of life? With a certain dexterity, one can obtain animation, a kind of warmth. With their lurches, efforts, jarring contrasts, surprises, small miracles, electric charges sometimes seem to surpass the action of life itself. The sign of true life is completely different: continuity. Born in one gush, it lasts, and grows placidly, slowly, *uno tenore*. Life's unity is not that of a little five-act play, but (in an often limitless development) the harmonic identity of soul.

The harshest critics, if they consider the totality of my book, will not fail to recognize in it these lofty conditions of life. It has not at all been rushed, abrupt; it had, at the very least, the quality of slowness. From the first to the last volume, the method is the same; as it is, in short, in my *Geography*, so it is in my *Louis XV*, and in my *Revolution*. No less rare in a labor of so many years, the form and the color are sustained. The same qualities, the same flaws. If the flaws had disappeared, the work would be heterogeneous, motley, it would have lost its personality. Such as it *is*, it is better for it to remain harmonious and a living whole.

When I began, a book of genius existed, Thierry's. Shrewd and penetrating, he was a discerning interpreter, a great chiseler, an admirable worker, but too enslaved to one master. This master, this tyrant, is the exclusive, systematic postulate of the permanence of races. All things considered, what makes this great book beautiful is that, in spite of this system, which could easily be seen as deterministic, one senses at all times the respiration deep down of a heart powerfully moved by hostility to fatalistic forces, to invasion, a heart full of the national soul and the right to liberty.

I greatly loved and admired him. However, shall I say it? Neither the material nor the spiritual approach was adequate for me in his book.

The physical element, the race, the common people who continue it, I thought, needed a good solid base under them, the soil, to support and nourish them. Without a geographic foundation, the common people, the historic actor, seem to walk on air as in those Chinese paintings in which there is no ground. And note that this ground is not only the theater of action. By means of food, climate, etc., it exerts influence in a hundred ways. As the nest, so the bird. As the fatherland, so the man.

Race, a strong and dominant factor in barbarian times, before the great childbirth of nations, becomes less tangible, weaker, and almost obliterated, in proportion as each nation fashions itself and becomes a person. The famous Mr. Mill says it very well: "It would be too easy to avoid the study of moral and social influences by attributing differences of character and of conduct, to innate, indestructible differences."[3]

Contrary to those who pursue this racial element and exaggerate its influence in modern times, I drew from history itself an enormous, and too little noticed, moral fact. It is the powerful *labor of oneself on oneself*, whereby France, by her own progress, transforms all her raw elements. From the Roman municipal element, from the Germanic tribes, from the Celtic clan — which have been annulled and have disappeared — we have produced in the course of time completely different results, results even contrary, to a great extent, to everything that preceded them.

Life exerts upon itself an action of self-gestation, which, from pre-existing materials, creates absolutely new things. From the bread, the fruits that I have eaten, I make red and salty blood which does not at all resemble the foods from which it is derived. So goes the historical life process, and so too goes each people fabricating itself, generating itself, grinding and amalgamating elements, which probably remain there as obscure and muddled ingredients, but which are relatively insignificant compared to the long, slow travail of the great soul.

France itself has formed France, and the deterministic element of race in this process seems to me secondary. France is the daughter of her freedom. It is the life force, which we call mankind, that plays the essential role in human progress.

---

3   This is the principal point on which I differ from my learned friend, M. Henri Martin. Moreover, this disagreement does not at all diminish my sympathetic esteem for his great and very beautiful *History of France*, which is so instructive, so enriched by his research and so full of ideas. It would have been infinitely useful, in reviving the all too unrecorded national tradition, for these two histories, which help and compensate for one another, to have appeared simultaneously.

To sum up, history, as I saw it represented by those eminent (in several cases admirable) men, still seemed unsubstantial in its two approaches:

Not material enough, taking races into account, but not the soil, the climate, foods, and so many physical and physiological conditions.

Not spiritual enough, speaking about laws, about political acts, but not about ideas, about customs, and not about the great progressive interior movement of the national soul.

Above all, not very interested in minute details of erudition, where what is most valuable, perhaps, remained buried in unpublished sources.

My life was in this book, it has been transformed into it. This book has been my life's only outcome. But is this identity of the book with its author not dangerous? Is not the work colored with the feelings, the times, of the person who produced it?

That is what always happens. No portrait is so exact, none so conforms to the model, that the artist has not added to it a little of himself. Our masters in history have not escaped from this law. Tacitus, in his *Tiberius*, also paints himself along with the suffocating atmosphere of his times, "the fifteen long years" of silence. Thierry, in recounting for us Klodowig, William and his conquest, reveals the inner breath, the excitement of a recently invaded France and his opposition to a regime he considered to be that of a foreigner.

If this be a flaw, we must admit that it is a very useful one. The historian who does not have it, who aims to disappear while writing, to not exist, to follow contemporary reports from behind (as Barante did for Froissart) is not an historian at all. The old chronicler, although quite charming, is absolutely incapable of telling the poor valet following at his heels, what is the great, the somber, the frightful fourteenth century. In order to know it, we need all our forces of analysis and erudition; we need a great device to help us pierce mysteries inaccessible to the simple storyteller. What is this device, what instrument is needed? It is the modern personality, so powerful and enlarged. In penetrating an object more and more deeply, we come to love it, and henceforth we examine it with growing interest. The heart touched with emotion has second sight; it sees a multitude of things invisible to those who are indifferent. History and the historian merge in this view. Is this good? Is this bad? Something is operating here that has not been described and that it is our duty to reveal.

It is a fact that history, in the progress of time, makes the historian much more than it is made by him. My book has created me. It is I who became its handiwork. The son has produced the father. If it first issued from me, from my storm of youth (which still rages), it has made me much stronger, more enlightened, even given me more fertile warmth, more actual power to resurrect the past. If my work resembles me, that is good. The traits which it shares with me are in a large part those which I owe to it, which I took from it.

My destiny has favored me well. I possessed two things which are rather rare, and which have produced this work.

First, freedom, which has been its soul.

Then, some useful obligations which, by slowing down, delaying its completion, made it more thoughtful, stronger, gave it solidity, the sturdy foundation of time.

I was free because of solitude, poverty and a simple life, and free through my teaching. Under the ministry of Martignac (a brief moment of generosity) it was decided to reconstitute the École Normale, and Monsieur Letronne, who was consulted, had the chair of philosophy and history given to me. My *Précis of Modern History*, my *Vico*, published in 1827, seemed to him sufficient qualifications. This dual teaching, which I carried on still later at the Collège de France, opened up a sphere of limitless freedom for me. My boundless domain included every fact, every idea.

My only master was Vico. His principle of the living force, of a *humanity that creates itself*, made both my book and my teaching.

I kept my distance from the majestic, sterile Doctrinaires, and from the great Romantic flood of "art for art's sake." I had my world within myself. I held my life within myself, as well as my renewals and my fecundity; but also my dangers. Which? My heart, my youth, my very method, and the new demand made of history: no longer just to recount or judge, but to *summon, remake, revive* the ages. To have enough passionate flame to reheat ashes long cold–that was the first point, and it was not without peril. But the second point, still more perilous perhaps, was to enter into an intimate relationship with the revived dead, and who knows? finally become one of them.

My first pages after the July Revolution, written on the burning cobblestones, were a vision of the world, of Universal History, as freedom's struggle, its ever-repeated victory over the world of determinism, in short, as an Eternal July.

With incredible energy, that little book [*Introduction to World History*] was carried forward in rapid flight on two wings at once (as always with me): Nature and Spirit, two interpretations of the vast general movement. My method was already in it. I said there in 1830 what I said (in *The Witch* [1862]) about Satan, the weird name of still youthful freedom, combative at first, and negative, but later creative and increasingly fruitful.

In 1829 Jouffroy had just uttered the keyword of the Restoration: "How dogmas come to an end." In July, the Church was deserted. No independent thinker would have doubted at that moment that Montesquieu's prophecy of the death of Catholicism was soon to be fulfilled.

I was in this respect perhaps the freest man in the world, having had the rare advantage of not having endured the deadly education which catches immature young souls, and immediately chloroforms them. For me the Church was a foreign world, an object of pure curiosity, like the moon. What I knew best about that pale star was that its days were numbered, that it did not have long to live. But who would replace it? Such was the question. The Church was caught up in the moral cholera that so closely followed the July Revolution, the disillusionment, and the loss of high hopes. There was a rapid downward movement. The novel, the theater burst forth with daring ugliness. Talent was plentiful, but the brutality was crude; this was not the fecund orgy of the old cults of nature which had its grandeur, but rather a deliberate intoxication with sterile materialism. Much bombast, and little beneath.

The founding text that preceded the July Revolution had been *Honor to Industry*, the new queen of the world, who overcomes, subjugates matter. After July, this was reversed: matter, in its turn, subjugated human energy.

This last fact is not rare in history. Nothing is older than this idea of the right of matter which demands to have its turn. But what made it shocking in the case of the Saint Simonians was the ugliness of a Janus,[4] retaining in its worship a servile imitation of the Catholic institution.

At a solemn meeting to which we were invited, Quinet and I saw with astonishment, in this religion of the bank, a remarkable return of what was supposed to have been abolished. We saw a clergy and a pope; we saw the preacher receive the transmission of Grace from this pope by the laying on of hands. He said: "Down with the cross!" But it was present in the sacerdotal authoritarian forms reminiscent of the Middle Ages. The old religion, which they claimed to combat, was being renewed at its worst; confession, spiritual direction, nothing was missing. The capuccini were

---

4   This has nothing to do with the honesty of the individuals. There were some admirable men, people like Bazart, Barrault, Carnot, Charton, D'Eichthal, Lemonnier, etc.

restored: bankers, industrialists. The bland suavity of a new Molinos had the odor of sweet Jesus.

Do away with the Middle Ages, fine. But they were plundering it. This was quite apparent to me. When I returned home, moved by a blind and generous impulse, I wrote forceful words in favor of that dying age which was being pillaged during its death agony. Those juvenile lines, foolish if you will, but doubtless excusable as a heartfelt emotion, hardly belonged in my little book inspired by the July Revolution and Freedom, by its victory over the clergy. They clashed strongly with Satan, whom this book introduces as a mythical figure of freedom. No matter. The lines are there, and they still make me laugh. Such apparent contradictions hardly bother a young artist of solid faith, but innocent, uncalculating, with little sense of the danger of being soft-hearted toward the enemy.

At that time I was an artist and a writer, much more than an historian. So it appears in the first two volumes (*France in the Middle Ages*). The documents which have thrown light on these shadows, on the abyss of these endless miseries had not yet been published. The great synthetic effect produced by these documents was, for me, that of a dismal harmony, a colossal symphony, whose countless dissonances reached my ear but faintly. This is a very serious flaw. Abelard's cry of Reason, the immense movement of 1200, so cruelly stifled, are not sufficiently present in these volumes; they have been sacrificed excessively to the artistic effect of the great unity.

And yet, today, having passed through so many years, ages, different worlds, as I reread this book and see its failings quite clearly, I say:

"It cannot be meddled with."

It was written in a state of rare, truly uncommon solitude, freedom, purity, and high mental tension. Its candor, its passion, the enormous quantity of life which animates it, pleaded to me in its favor, defending it against my scrutiny. The rectitude of youth is felt in its very errors. Its broad general objectives were, on the whole, attained. For the first time France's soul appears in its vivid personality, while no less the Church's impotence is exposed in fullest light.

A radical impotence, twice confirmed.

In the first volume the Church, queen under Dagobert and under the Carlovingians, is seen to be incapable of doing anything for the world, for the social order.

In the second volume, having produced a king-priest, a king-abbot, having made a canon of her eldest son, the king of France, the Church is seen crushing her enemies (1200), smothering the free Spirit, bringing about no moral reform. Finally, eclipsed, overtaken by Saint Louis, the Church is (before 1300) subordinated, dominated by the State.

That is the portion of those two volumes that is unquestionably true to reality. But in the portion due to mirage, to poetic illusion, can it be said that all is false? No.

That latter aspect expresses the idea that such an age had of itself, tells of what it dreamed and desired. It represents the age truthfully in its aspirations, in its deep sadness, in the reverie that kept it transfixed before the Church, weeping beneath its stone niches, sighing, waiting for what never comes.

It was necessary to recover the idea that the Middle Ages had of itself, to reproduce its impulse, its desire, its soul, before judging it. Who was destined to rediscover its soul? Our great writers, evidently, for they all had a Catholic education. How then can it be that these geniuses, so well prepared for this, walked around the Church without entering, so to speak, without fathoming what was inside? Some seek the themes of their melodies in the echoes of church entrances or cloisters. Others, with great effort and a powerful chisel, excavate the ornaments, arm the towers, the roofs, with formidable masks, with gnomes and grimacing devils. But all that is not the Church herself. Let us first remake her.

The odd thing is that the only person with enough love to recreate, to remake the Church's inner world, is the one whom she did not raise at all, *who never entered into communion with her,* who had no faith other than in humanity itself, no imposed creed, nothing but a free mind.

This mind approached the dead thing with a human sensitivity, with the great advantage of not having had to pass by way of the priests and the ponderous formulas that buried the Middle Ages. The incantation of an established ritual would have accomplished nothing. Everything would have remained as cold as ashes. And, moreover, if history had arrived with all its critical severity, imposing absolute justice, I do not know if those dead would have dared to come back to life. They would, rather, have remained hiding in their tombs.

I had a fine disease which clouded my youth, but which was well suited to an historian. I loved death. I had lived for nine years at the gates of the Père-Lachaise cemetery, which was at that time the only place where I could take a walk. Then I lived near the Bièvre district of Paris, amidst large gardens adjoining convents, another kind of sepulcher. I led a life which the world could have described as a buried one, having no company other than the past, and for friends, entombed peoples. By recreating their legends, I awakened in them a multitude of vanished things. Certain nurses' songs of which I held the secret had a sure effect. By my tone of voice they believed I was one of them. I was given the gift that Saint Louis requests and does not obtain: "The gift of tears."

A powerful, extremely fruitful gift. All those for whom I wept, peoples and gods, lived again. This naïve magic had an almost infallible power of evocation. Egypt, for example, had been spelled out, deciphered, all its tombs excavated, but its soul had not been rediscovered. For some the key lay in the climate, for others in certain symbols of vacuous subtlety. I myself found it in the heart of Isis, in the sufferings of the common people, the eternal mourning and the eternal wound of the fellah's family, in his insecure life, in the captivities, the razzias of Africa, the great trade in men, from Nubia to Syria. Man seized and carried off far away, bound to hard labor, *man made into a tree* or tied to a tree, nailed, mutilated, dismembered, that is the universal Agony of so many gods (Osiris, Adonis, Iacchus, Athis, etc.). How many Christs, and how many Calvaries! How many funereal laments! How many tears all along the way! (See my little *Bible[of Humanity]*, 1864).

I had no other art in 1833. One teardrop, one only, cast onto the foundation of the gothic Church, sufficed to summon it forth. Something human surged from it, the blood of legend, and, borne up by that powerful spurt, everything rose to the sky. From inside to outside, everything sprang out in blossoms—of stone? No, blossoms of life.—Sculpt them? Approach them with iron and chisel? That would have horrified me, and I would have expected to see them bleed!

Would you like to know why I was so sensitive to these gods? It is because they die. They all depart in their turn. Each one, just like us, having received a little holy water and tears, descends into the pyramids, the hypogeum, the catacombs, etc. Alas! What ever returns from there? I will not deny that *"after three days"* (each one three thousand years long), a slight breath might reappear. The Indian soul has not vanished from the earth; it returns in the love it had for all life. Egypt has always echoed in this world in the love of death and the hope of immortality. The delicate Christian soul, in its sweetness, can probably never expire without return. Its legend has perished, but that is not enough. It must cast off the terrifying injustice (Grace, Arbitrary Judgment) which is its vital center, its heart, the true basis of its dogma. It will be hard, but Christianity must die in those very principles, openly accept penitence, purification, and expiation by death.

Wise men told me: "It is not safe to live to this extent in such intimacy with the other world. The dead are all so kind! All these creatures, which have become so peaceful and gentle, have strange powers of extravagant illusion. Among them you will be caught up in strange dreams, and, who knows? develop attachments. Whoever dwells there for too long becomes livid from it. You risk coming upon the white Fiancée, pale and charming, who drinks your heart's blood! Follow at least the example of Aeneas, who did not venture among the dead without a sword in his hand in order to drive away these images and not get too close to them (*Ferro diverberat umbras*)."

A sword! Dismal advice. What! When those beloved images approached me seeking to live, I should have harshly thrust them aside! What doleful wisdom! ... Oh! How completely ignorant philosophers are of the true essence of the artist, of the secret talisman that constitutes the power of history and enables the historian to pass time and again among the dead!

I would have you know, then, ignorant ones, that, unarmed, without a sword, without arguing with those trustful souls who are begging for resurrection, art, while welcoming them and restoring their life's breath, art nevertheless retains its full lucidity. I do not mean irony, in which many have placed the essence of art. Rather I am speaking of the mighty duality which permits one, while loving them, to see nonetheless what they are, "that they are the dead."

The world's greatest artists, the geniuses who examine nature with such tender love, will allow me to make here a humble comparison. Have you sometimes seen the touching seriousness of a young girl, innocent, and yet deeply affected by her future motherhood, who cradles the work of her hands, animates it with her kisses, says to it from her heart: My daughter! ... If you touch her work roughly, she becomes upset and screams. But this does not prevent her from knowing deep down who this being is that she animates, enables to talk and to reason, vivifies with her soul.

This is a small image of a great thing. It is precisely art at its moment of conception. Such is the essential condition of artistic creativity. It is love, but also a smile. It is this loving smile that creates.

If the smile is left behind, if irony begins, along with harsh criticism and logic, then life becomes chilled, withdraws, contracts, and nothing is produced at all. Weak and sterile people who, even as they try to produce something, fill their wretched offspring with *althoughs* and *nisis*, these solemn idiots do not understand that no life emerges from a frigid environment; from their glacial nothingness will issue, , , nothingness.

Death can appear at the moment of love, in the creative surge. But in that case let it be with infinite tenderness, with tears and pity (which still express love). In the intensely emotional moments when I incubated and reproduced the life of the Christian Church, I announced unequivocally the sentence of its impending death. I was also filled with pity for it. Recreating it through art, I told the invalid what Hezekiah asked of God. Nothing more. Conclude that I am Catholic! What could be more inane! The believer does not say the Office of the Dead for a person in the throes of death whom he believes to be eternal.

These two volumes were successful and accepted by the public. I was the first to have established France as a person. Less exclusive than Thierry, and subordinating the element of race, I strongly underlined the geographic principle of local influences, and along with that, the shared labor of the entire nation in creating, fabricating itself. In my blind enthusiasm for the Gothic I had caused the stone to give forth blood, and the Church to flower, to rise up like the flower of legend. This pleased the public. It pleased me a good deal less. That work shone like a great flame. I found too much subtlety in it, too much wit, too much system.

Four whole years went by before the third volume (which begins around 1300). In preparing it I tried to extend myself, to become deeper, to be more *human*, simpler. I sat for some time in Luther's house, collecting his table talk, such strong, virile, and touching words, which slipped from this heroic fellow (1834). But nothing was more useful to me than Grimm's colossal book, his *Antiquities of German Law*. A very difficult book which sets forth the symbols and the formulas—found in all the dialects and all the periods of that language—with which the various, so diverse Germanies have sanctified the great events of human life (birth, marriage, and death, testaments, sales, tributes, etc.). Some day I will describe the incredible passion with which I ventured to understand and translate this book. I didn't shut myself up in it. From nation to nation, I went about collecting from everywhere, I went from the Indus to Ireland, from the Vedas and

Zoroaster up to the present, amassing these primitive formulas in which humanity so naïvely reveals so many intimate and profound things (1837).

This made another man of me. A strange inner transformation took place; it seemed to me that up until then, harsh and subtle, I was old, and that little by little, under the influence of that young humanity, I too became young. Refreshed by those living springs, my heart became a flower garden, as if touched by the morning dew. Oh! The dawn! Oh! Sweet childhood! Oh! Good and natural nature! What vigor this created within me, after the witherings of my mystic subtlety! How meager that Byzantine poetry now appeared to me, how sickly and barren, how emaciated! Yet I spared it still. But how shabby it appeared to me in the presence of humanity! This humanity I possessed, held firm, embraced in the very rich detail of its boundless variety (leafy as the forests of India, where each tree is a forest); and, looking down from above, I saw its sweet, mild harmony in which nothing is stifled; I seized the divine element in its worshipful unity.

Being so richly nourished and watered by nature, my substance expanding, I experienced an immense increase of solidity in my art, and (shall I say it? But it is true) an increase of kindness, and a heedlessness, an absolute ignorance of rivalries,—consequently a vast sympathy for mankind (which I scarcely saw) and for society, the world (which I never frequented).

I enjoyed the security of a body which had become firm and strong, in which good food changed and replaced—atom by atom, molecule by molecule—everything that had at first been weak. I was not the least bit affected by the malicious barbs of the Doctrinaires. I was no less indifferent to the ambushes of the Catholics. Everything I was collecting (involuntarily, without any thought of them), those unquestionable, countless facts, those mountains of truths which, in my persistent work, rose, pushed higher each day, all that was against them. None of them could have imagined the solid, deep foundation that I found there, so that I had neither the need nor the idea of polemics. My strength made my peace. It would have taken them ten thousand years to understand that what to them seemed weakness, the gentle, peaceful *human sense*, which was growing in me, was precisely my strength and what distanced me from them.[5]

---

5 As they sniff out death very well, those moments when the wounded soul might weaken, one of them, seductive and shrewd, came to see me at a time when I had had a painful loss in the family, and sounded me out. I was surprised, disconcerted by the idea that he could believe he had some hold on me, that he could say that we might reach an

The mongrel, half-Catholic salons, in the insipid atmosphere of the friends of Chateaubriand, might have been a more dangerous trap for me. The benevolent and pleasant Ballanche, then Monsieur de Lamartine, wanted to escort me several times to L'Abbaye-aux-Bois. I was perfectly aware that such surroundings, where everything was circumspect and decorous, would have civilized me too much. I had but one single strength, my savage virginity of opinion, and the free manner of an art which was all my own and new. I would have had to adapt myself, become milder, better mannered than was suitable for me. From that period on the salons were very hostile toward me. In them, Doctrinaires and Catholics have steadfastly waged war on me, attacking me less in particulars, praising me in order to destroy me and to deprive me of any authority: "He is a writer, a poet, a man of imagination."

This began at the time when I was the first to remove history from the vagueness which satisfied them; I established history from records, manuscripts, the enormous investigation of thousands of diverse documents.

No historian that I know of, before the publication of my third volume (a simple thing to verify), had used unpublished items. This began with the use I made in my history of the mysterious register of the *Interrogatory of the Temple*, which had been locked up for four hundred years, hidden, walled up, prohibited under the severest penalties, in the Treasury of the Cathedral, whence it was taken by the Harlays, then came to Saint-Germain-des-Prés, then to the National Library. The *Chronicles of Duguesclin*, then unpublished, also helped me. The enormous repository in the Archives provided me with a multitude of records which confirmed these manuscripts, and which were relevant to many other topics. This was the first time history had so serious a foundation.

What would have become of me, in studying the fourteenth century, if, clinging to the methods of my most illustrious predecessors, I had made myself the docile interpreter, the servile translator of the narratives of the time? Entering centuries rich in records and genuine documents, history

---

understanding, the differences between us being slight, etc. I spoke to him in these very words: "Monsignor, have you ever been on the sea of ice?" "Yes," he answered. "Have you ever seen a certain crack, over which, from one side to the other, one can speak, converse?" "Yes." "But you have not seen that this crack is an abyss...," I continued, "and so much so, Monsignor, so deep, that through the ice and the earth, it descends without anyone's ever having discovered the bottom. It goes as far as the center of the globe, continues across the globe, and is lost in the infinite."

came of age, acquired mastery of the chronicles which it controlled, purified and judged. Armed with unassailable documents unknown to these chronicles, history, as it were, held them on its knees like a little child to whose prattle it listens willingly, but whom it must often admonish and contradict.

One example, the one I suggested above, will suffice to make me understood. In the pleasant history in which Monsieur de Barante follows our story-tellers, Froissart, etc., so faithfully, step by step, it would seem that he cannot go too far wrong in clinging to these contemporaries. But then in examining the records, the various documents, so dispersed at the time though collected today, we recognize that the chronicler failed to appreciate, was unmindful of the broad features of the age. This is already a financial and juridical century in feudal form. It is often Pathelin masked as Arthur. The advent of gold, of the Jew, the weaving industry of Flanders, the dominant wool trade in England and Flanders—this is what allowed the English to prevail with regular troops, some of whom were hired and paid mercenaries. The *economic* revolution alone made the *military* revolution possible, which, through the punitive defeat of feudal knighthood, prepared, then brought about the *political* revolution. The tournaments of Froissart, Monstrelet, and the Golden Fleece have little influence in all this. They are completely incidental.

From that time on (1837), from volume to volume, I provided references to, and often quoted, manuscripts whose importance I explained and which were later published.

With such support, superior to all chronicles, history moves on, serious and strong, with authority. But independently of these specific instruments, acts and documents, immeasurable assistance arrives from everywhere. — Thousands of indirect revelations, whose outline illuminates the central narrative, come to it from literature and art, from commerce. —History becomes a reality guaranteed by the various verifications furnished by all the various forms of our activity.

Here again I am compelled to state it: I was alone. There hardly existed anything other than political history, government decrees and records, to a slight extent those of institutions. No one took into account that which accompanies, explains, and in part establishes that political history—social, economic, industrial conditions, those of literature and of ideas.

The third volume (1300-1400) examines all aspects of one century. It is not without weaknesses. It does not explain how 1300 was the atonement for 1200, how Boniface VIII paid for Innocent III. It is harsh, excessively so, toward the legists, toward the courageous men who slapped the face of the idol with the Albigensian hand of the valiant Nogaret. However, this volume is new and strong in deriving history principally from *the economic Revolution*, from the advent of gold, of the Jew and of Satan (the king of hidden treasures). It vigorously presents the very *mercantile* character of the times.

How England and Flanders were married by wool and cloth, how England drank Flanders, became saturated with her, enticing at any price the weavers driven out by the brutalities of the house of Bourbon: this is the great fact. An enriched England defeats us at Crécy, Poitiers, and Agincourt, with well-regulated troops which bury chivalry. A great social revolution.

The Black Plague, St. Vitus' dance, the flagellants and the witches' sabbath, those carnivals of despair impel the abandoned, leaderless people to act for themselves. The genius of France in her Danton of the time, Étienne Marcel, in her Paris, her Estates General, bursts forth unexpectedly in her constitution, admirable in its precocity, postponed, rubbed out by the petty, negative prudence of Charles V. Nothing has been cured. Aggravated, on the contrary, evil arrives at its culminating frenzy, the raging madness of Charles VI.

I have defined history as *Resurrection*. If that was ever realized, it happened in volume four (Charles VI). Perhaps, in fact, that is saying too much. This volume was created in a spurt of agony, in an ecstasy of that soul of yore, savage, sensual, and violent, cruel and tender, raging. As in *The Witch*, it is diabolical in some places, the dead dance there—not to provoke laughter as in Holbein's ironies, but in a painful frenzy in which one participates and gets caught up almost by merely observing it. It whirls with astonishing speed, a horrible rout. And we are breathless. No stopping, no distraction. Everywhere there is an emotional and deep basso continuo; beneath it all, there sounds a mysterious rolling, a muted thunder of the heart.

In the midst of so many gloomy things, we fall upon a great light—death enthroned in the Louvre—in a deserted Paris, the real death of France in the shape of the Englishman, of Lancaster. Henry, the king of priests, the damned Pharisee, tells us: "that we have perished only for our sins."

I do not answer him; let the English answer him themselves.

They say that before the battle of Agincourt, each Englishman looked to his salvation, made confession; the French embraced, forgave each other, and forgot their hatreds.

They say that in Spain where the French and English were waging war, the latter dying of hunger, the French fed them. I will not go beyond that: it is God's choice.

The greatest legend of our time is soon to come. It is seen in a frightful seed sprouting around 1360, sublime, charming, touching, and which flourishes in 1430 (third and fifth volumes).

France had glimpsed the town and its communes. But what about the countryside? Who knows about it before the fourteenth century? That vast world of shadows, those countless, ignored masses, break through one morning. In the third volume (mostly erudition), I was not on guard, expecting nothing, when the shape of Jacques, rising up on a furrow, blocked my path; a monstrous and frightful shape. I felt a convulsive contraction in my heart... Great God! Is this my father? The man of the Middle Ages?... "Yes," he answered, "Look how I am made! Behold a thousand years of sorrows..." Those sorrows, I felt them immediately as they flowed up into me from the depths of time... It was he, it was I (same soul and same person) who had endured all this... From these thousand years, a tear came to me, burning, as heavy as a world, which pierced the page. No one (friend, enemy) passed through them without weeping.

The form was dreadful, but the voice was tender. With this my pain increased. Beneath this frightening mask was a human soul. Deep, cruel mystery. It cannot be understood without going back a little.

Saint Francis, a child who does not know what he says, and who speaks the better for it, tells those who ask who wrote *The Imitation of Christ*: "The author is the Holy Spirit."

"The Holy Spirit," says Joachim de Flores, "is the spirit *whose reign arrives after the reign of Jesus.*"

It is the spirit of union, of love, finally emerging from the suffocation of legend. The free associations of fraternities and free towns were for the most part moved by this spirit. Such was, in 1200, in the time of the Albigensians, the religion both of the free towns and of the knights of southern France, a religion in a new spirit that the Church drowned in torrents of blood. And so the Spirit, frail dove, seems to perish, to disappear. From that moment on it becomes airborne, and will be breathed in everywhere.

Even in that little book, *The Imitation of Christ*, so monastic and devout, you find passages of absolute solitude in which the Spirit strikingly replaces everything, in which nothing is seen any more, neither priest nor Church. If one hears its inward voices in the convents, how much more so in the forests, in the free boundless Church! It was the Spirit speaking, from deep within the oaks, when Joan of Arc heard it, shuddered, and said tenderly: "My voices!"

Holy voices, voices of conscience, which Joan of Arc carries with her into battles, into prisons, against the English, against the Church. There the world is changed. The passive resignation of Christians (so useful to tyrants) is superseded by the heroic tenderness which takes our afflictions to heart, which wants to set God's justice here below, a justice that acts, that fights, that saves and heals.

Who worked that miracle, so contrary to the Gospels? A superior love, *love in action,* love unto death, "the pity which was in the kingdom of France."

How divine a spectacle when, on the scaffold, the girl, abandoned and alone, upholds her interior Church against the priest-king, against the murderous Church, in the midst of the flames, and takes flight saying: "My voices!"

This point is one in which I should observe how much my history, so glibly accused of being "poetry," of being "passion," has on the contrary retained its solidity and lucidity, even in emotional areas where it might perhaps be excusable to shut one's eyes. Everyone has hesitated at the Joan of Arc story, seeing through their tears the flames of the pyre. While I was assuredly moved, I still saw clearly, and I noticed two things:

1) The innocent heroine, without being aware of it, did much more than liberate France, she liberated the future by establishing the new standard, the opposite of Christian passivity. The modern hero *is the hero of action.* The deadly doctrine, which our friend Renan still praises excessively, of passive, interior freedom, preoccupied with itself and its own salvation, preoccupied with protecting itself, and which hands the world over to Evil and, abandons it to Tyrants, that doctrine breathes its last on the pyre at Rouen, and in a mystic form foretells the French Revolution.

2) In this grand narrative I have practiced and demonstrated something new, from which the young might benefit: it is the fact that *the historical method* is often the opposite of *specifically literary art.* The writer busied with trying to increase his effects, to make things stand out, almost always likes

to surprise, to seize the reader, to make him exclaim: "Ah!" The writer is happy if the natural event appears miraculous. On the contrary, the historian's special mission is to explain whatever appears miraculous, to surround it with the precedents and circumstances leading up to it, to bring it back to nature. Here, I should say, I deserved credit. In admiring, in loving this sublime personality, I have shown how natural she was.

The sublime is not at all outside nature; it is, on the contrary, the moment at which nature is most itself, in its natural height and depth. In the fourteenth and fifteenth centuries, in their excessive miseries, in their horrible extremities, the heart grows larger. The crowd is a hero. There were in those times many Joans of Arc, at least as regards courage. I meet many of them along my way: example, the fourteenth-century peasant, the Grand Ferré; example, in the fifteenth century, Jeanne Hachette who defends and saves Beauvais. Such naïve heroes often appear to me in the histories of our free towns.

I have told the facts quite plainly. From the time the English lost their mainstay, the Duke of Burgundy, they became quite weak. On the contrary, the French, rallying their armed forces of the South, became extremely strong. But this produced no harmony. The charming personality of this young peasant girl, with her tender, emotional, and joyous heart (heroic gaiety burst forth in all her answers), became a center and she united everything. She acted effectively because she had no art, no magic, no enchantments, no miracles. All her power is humanity. She has no wings, this poor angel; she is the common people, she is weak, she is us, she is everyone.

In the lonely galleries of the Archives where I wandered for twenty years, in that deep silence, murmurs nevertheless would reach my ears. The distant sufferings of so many souls, stifled in those ancient times, would moan softly. Stern reality protested against art, and occasionally had bitter words for it: "What are you fooling around with? Are you another Walter Scott, recounting picturesque details at great length, the sumptuous meals of Philip the Good, the empty Oath of the Pheasant? Do you know that our martyrs have been expecting you for four hundred years? Do you know that the valiant men of Courtray, of Rosebecque, do not have the monument which history owed them? The salaried chroniclers, Froissart the chaplain, Monstrelet the chatterbox, do not suffice. It was with firm faith, with the hope of justice that they gave their lives. They would have the right to say, 'History! Settle with us! Your creditors are summoning you! We accepted death for one line from you!'"

What did I owe them? To tell the story of their battles, to enter their ranks, to go halves with them in victory or defeat? That was not enough. For my ten years of strenuous perseverance when I reproduced the struggle of the Northern Towns, I undertook much more. I redid everything from top to bottom so as to restore their life to them, their arts, especially their rights.

First, the right which these cities had over their surrounding countryside; that was the most sacred of rights, for they had created the land itself, reclaimed it from the water, constructed the canals that are the life, the defense, and the communications system of the region. These cities produced and created. Their masters have destroyed. How pallid that world, so lively then, is today! What is the whole of Belgium compared with Ghent or Bruges, compared with that Liège of former days, from which each of them launched armies?

I plunged into the common people. While Olivier de la Marche and Chastellain were lolling about at the meals of the Golden Fleece, I probed the wine cellars where Flanders was fermenting, with her masses of valiant workers and mystics. I devoutly restored everything, their powerful *Friendships* (as they called their communes), their *Candid Truths* (the name of their meetings), without neglecting their bells, and their brotherly chimes. I put the dreaded Roelandt back into his tower, my great bronze friend whose solemn voice, ringing out for ten leagues, made John the Fearless and Charles the Bold quake.

One quite essential point, which contemporaries as well as our modern writers neglect, is to distinguish sharply, to characterize the particular personality of each city. Therein lies, however, the true reality, the charm of this so diversified country. I clung to that task; it was a religion for me to reconstruct the soul of each of those old and cherished cities, and that could be done only by showing clearly how each trade and each way of life created a race of workers. I set Ghent aside, that deep hive of battles, with its brave and devout weavers. I also set Bruges aside, so great and so appealing, with the seventeen nations of its merchants and the three hundred painters who made an Italy in one city. And Ypres, the Pompeii of Flanders, today deserted, which preserves its true monument, the prodigious market place of all trades, this cathedral of labor where every good worker should remove his hat.

The conflagration of Dinant, the cruel end of Liège, close this history of the Free Towns with a heartbreaking tragedy. Myself a child of the Meuse on my mother's side, I had a family involvement with it. Those poor French nations, lost in the Ardennes, between hostile peoples and competing languages, moved me greatly. I gave back to the people of Liège the great renovator, Van Eyck, who transformed painting. I discovered, I exhumed from the ashes of Dinant its lost arts, so dear to the Middle Ages—humble and deeply touching arts that were the loyal servants, the household friends of all Europe.

How can I thank my friends, my avengers, the good Swiss chroniclers who luckily arrive with their hunting horns, and spears, at the great hunt of Morat, and who bring to bay the wild boar, that cruel beast, Charles the Bold? Their narratives are heroically cheerful songs. It is a pleasure to see this frightful swelling bombast punctured, suddenly flattened. One undeniably favors Louis XI in his tricky struggle against barbaric pride, feudal brutality. He is a fox who nets the fake lion. At least the spirit triumphs. The refined and firm prose of Commynes overcomes coarse rhetoric, counterfeit knighthood. An irony, still petty and malicious, worthy of the medieval fabliaux, appears here in history. Tomorrow, strong and powerful, history will become fruitful in the great days of the Renaissance.

That good king, Louis XI, held me up for a very long time. My entire fifteenth century came forth from records and documents. The extremely vast work of Legrand nonetheless requires verification of his often very inexact transcriptions against the originals (Gaignières, etc.), a labor requiring great patience.

Through Louis XI I entered the centuries of monarchy. I was about to undertake this study when an accident made me reflect deeply. One day, passing through Reims, I examined in great detail the magnificent cathedral, the splendid church of the Coronation.

The interior cornice on which you can walk around the church at a height of eighty feet, makes it appear enchanting, of floral richness, a permanent hallelujah. In the hollow vastness, you still seem to hear the great official hubbub that was said to be the voice of the people. At the windows you seem to see the birds that were released when the clergy, anointing the king, made the pact between Throne and Altar. Returning outside over the arches in the immense panorama which embraces all of Champagne, I came to the last small steeple, exactly above the chancel. There a strange scene greatly amazed me. The round tower was wreathed with tortured criminals. One has a rope around his neck. Another has lost an ear. The injured are more wretched there than the dead. How right they are! What a frightful contrast! What! The church of festivals, this bride, has taken this gloomy ornament as a wedding necklace! This pillory of the common people is set above the altar. But could not their tears, through the arches, have fallen upon the heads of kings! Fearful anointing of the Revolution, of God's anger! "I cannot understand the centuries of monarchy if first, above all, I do not establish within myself the soul and the faith of the common people." That is what I said to myself, and, after Louis XI, I wrote *The Revolution* (1845-1853).

Readers were taken aback, but nothing made more sense than that. After many ordeals which I have recounted elsewhere and through which I saw the other shore closely, having died and been reborn, with centupled strength I produced the *Renaissance*. When I returned, looked back and reexamined my Middle Ages, that splendid sea of folly, I was seized with a violent hilarity, and with the sixteenth and seventeenth centuries I had a terrific celebration. Rabelais and Voltaire laughed in their graves. The broken gods, the rotten kings, appeared without any covering. The insipid history of conventional clichés, that shameful prude with which people were content, disappeared. From the Medicis to Louis XIV a harsh autopsy set forth the character of this government of corpses (1855-1868).

Such a history was certain of one success, offending every friend of falsehood. But that includes many people, particularly those in positions of authority. Priests and royalists howled. The Doctrinaires did their best to smile.

These reactions made very little difference to that patient history. It is strong, solid, well founded, and it will wait for its time to come.

In my series of Prefaces, and my Explanatory Notes, can be seen, from volume to volume, the foundation underneath, the enormous underpinning of documents and manuscripts, of rare publications, etc., which sustains it.[6]

---

6   I do not want to anticipate here. In only one or two words I can say: It is this book, "this book of a poet and a man of imagination," that, thanks to its telling documentation, has told everyone whatever was important to them:

To the Protestants, the essential fact of the Saint-Bartholomew's Day Massacre toils fifteen days before in Brussels (Granvelle papers, 10 August). Then, so many facts about the Revocation of the Edict of Nantes, on which they themselves had thrown very little light.

To the Royalists, a whole world of odd anecdotal facts; for example, the legend of the *Man in the Iron Mask* and the wisdom of their queen. Franklin's letters (1863) revealed the secret, according to Richelieu, and have proven that I alone was right.

To the financiers, Law's system (unexplained by M. Thiers in 1826) is finally elucidated,

That is how forty years went by. I hardly suspected it when I began. I believed I was going to write an abridged history of a few volumes in perhaps four years, in six years. But one can abridge only what is well known. And neither I myself, nor anyone, knew that history.

After just my first two volumes, I caught a glimpse of the immense perspectives of this *terra incognita*. I said: "It will take ten years..." No, twenty; no, thirty... And the road ahead of me grew longer and longer. I did not complain. On exploratory voyages one's heart enlarges, grows, no longer sees anything but the goal. One forgets oneself entirely. So it happened with me. My fervent pursuit constantly pushing me forward, I lost sight of myself, I withdrew from myself. I let the world pass me by, and I took history for life.

And now it has slipped away. I regret nothing. I ask for nothing. Well, what would I ask for, beloved France, with whom I have lived, whom I leave with such deep regret! In what companionship I have spent forty years (ten centuries) with you! We shared so many impassioned, noble, arduous hours, often in winter too, before the dawn! So many days of hard work and studies in the depths of the Archives! I worked for you, I went, came, searched, wrote. Each day I gave everything of myself, perhaps even more. The next morning, finding you at my table, I believed myself identical with you, strong with your powerful life and your eternal youth.

But how, having enjoyed the remarkable fortune of such companionship, having lived for long years through your great soul, how have I not benefited more within myself? Oh! The answer is that, in order to restore all this for you I have had to tread again that long path of misery, strewn with cruel adventures, hundreds of diseased and deadly things. I have drunk too much bitterness. I have swallowed too many plagues, too many vipers, and too many kings.

Very well! My great France, if in order to retrieve your life, a man had to surrender himself, to cross again and again, so many times, the river of death, he does not regret it, he thanks you still. And his greatest sorrow is that he must leave you here.

Paris, 1870.

---

both by manuscripts and by the history of the Paris and London Stock Exchanges.

As for the Revolution, what can I say? Mine emerged entirely from the three great archive collections of our times which are in Paris. Could Louis Blanc (despite his merit and his talent, for which I have great respect) have perceived the nature of the Revolution? Could he have recreated it in London with the help of a few brochures? I cannot believe it. Read, moreover, and compare.

6. Select Bibliography of Critical Writings on Michelet

Barthes, Roland. *Michelet par lui-même* (Paris: Éditions du Seuil, 1969).

—. *Michelet*, translated by Richard Howard (New York: Hill and Wang, 1987).

Bernard-Griffiths, Simone, ed. *Variétés sur Michelet* (Saint-Genouph: Nizet, 1998; Cahiers Romantiques, 3). Essays by Pascale Auraix-Jonchière, Ceri Crossley, Bernard-Griffiths, Pierre Laforgue, Louis Le Guilloux, Muriel Louâpre, Paule Petitier, Laudyce Rétat, Paul Viallaneix.

Brahm, Alcanter de. *Michelet inconnu* (Paris: Debresse, 1937).

Braudel, Fernand. *Écrits sur l'histoire* (Paris: Flamarion, 1969).

Calo, Jeanne. *La Création de la femme chez Michelet* (Paris: Nizet, 1975).

Chabaud, Alfred. *Jules Michelet. Son oeuvre, portrait et autographe* (Paris: Éditions de la Nouvelle Revue Critique, 1929).

Cornuz, Jeanlouis. *Jules Michelet. Un Aspect de la pensée religieuse au XIXᵉ siècle.* (Geneva: Droz; Lille: Giard, 1955).

Corréard, F. *Michelet* (Paris: H. Lecène and H. Oudin, 1888).

Crossley, Ceri. *French Historians and Romanticism* (London: Routledge, 1993).

Febvre, Lucien. *Michelet 1798-1874* (Geneva: Éditions des Trois Collines, 1946).

—. *Michelet et la Renaissance* (Paris: Flammarion, 1992).

Gossman, Lionel. "The Go-Between: Jules Michelet, 1798-1874," *Modern Language Notes* 89 (1974): 503-541.

—. Foreword, special number on Jules Michelet, *Clio* 6, no. 2 (1977): 121-129.

—. "Jules Michelet and Romantic Historiography," in *Scribner's European Writers*, ed. Jacques Barzun and George Stade (New York: Charles Scribner's Sons, 1985), vol. 5, pp. 571-606.

—. "Michelet and the French Revolution," in *The French Revolution and the Creation of Modern Political Culture*, ed. François Furet and Mona Ozouf (Oxford: Pergamon Press, 1989), vol. 3, pp. 639-663.

—. "Michelet," in *The New Oxford Companion to Literature in French*, ed. Peter France (Oxford: Clarendon Press, 1995), pp. 524-526.

—. "Jules Michelet: histoire nationale, biographie, autobiographie," *Littérature* 102 (May 1996): 29-54.

—. "Michelet and Natural History: The Alibi of Nature," *Proceedings of the American Philosophical Society* 145 (2001): 283-333.

Guehenno, Jean. *L'Évangile éternel. Étude sur Michelet* (Paris: Grasset, 1927).

Haac, Oscar. *Les Principes inspirateurs de Michelet* (New Haven: Yale University Press; Paris: P.U.F., 1951).

—. *Jules Michelet* (Boston: Twayne, 1982).

Halévy, Daniel. *Jules Michelet* (Paris: Hachette, 1928).

Kaegi, Werner. *Michelet und Deutschland* (Basel: Schwabe, 1936).

Kaplan, Edward K. "Les Deux sexes de l'esprit: Michelet phénoménologue de la pensée créatrice et morale," *Europe* 535-536 (November-December 1973): 97-111.

—. "Michelet évolutionniste," in *Michelet Cent Ans Après*, ed. Paul Viallaneix (Grenoble: Presses Universitaires de Grenoble, 1975), pp. 111-128.

—. "Le Symbolisme de la nature chez Michelet: Introduction littéraire à son spiritualisme," *Nineteenth Century French Studies* 3, no. 3-4 (Spring-Summer 1975): 141-164.

—. "Michelet's Revolutionary Symbolism: From Hermeneutics to Politics," *The French Review* 50, no. 5 (April 1977): 713-723.

—. *Michelet's Poetic Vision: A Romantic Philosophy of Nature, Man & Woman* (Amherst: University of Massachusetts Press, 1977).

—. *Mother Death. The Journal of Jules Michelet, 1815-1850* (Amherst: University of Massachusetts Press, 1984).

—. "La Spiritualité de Michelet: Une nouvelle religion républicaine?" *Littérature et Nation* 18 (1997): 205-221.

—. "L'Internet de Michelet: Evolution, Immortalité, Fragilité du Moi," *Europe* 829 (May 1998): 128-137.

—. "La Religion écologiste de Michelet: catéchisme, hagiographie, communion," *Michelet entre naissance et renaissance: 1798-1998* (Clermont-Ferrand: Presses Universitaires Blaise Pascal, 2001): 77-92.

Kippur, Stephen A. *Jules Michelet, A Study of Mind and Sensibility* (Albany, N.Y.: SUNY Press, 1981).

Kogan, Vivian. *The "I" of History. Self-Fashioning and National Consciousness in Jules Michelet* (Chapel Hill, N.C.: Department of Romance Languages, University of North Carolina, 2006; North Carolina Studies in the Romance Languages and Literatures, no. 286).

Michelet, Jules. *Correspondance générale*, ed. Louis Le Guillou, 12 vols. (Paris: Champion, 1994-2001).

—. *Ecrits de jeunesse: Journal (1820-1823), Mémorial, Journal des idées*, ed. Paul Viallaneix (Paris: Gallimard, 1959).

—. *Lettres inédites à Alfred Dumesnil et à Eugène Noël (1841-1871)*, ed. Paul Sirven (Paris: Presses Universitaires de France, 1924).

—.*Oeuvres complètes*, ed. Paul Viallaneix, 21 vols. (Paris: Flammarion, 1971-1987).

Mitzman, Arthur. *Michelet, Historian. Rebirth and Romanticism in Nineteenth-Century France* (New Haven: Yale University Press, 1990).

—. *Michelet ou la subversion du passé. Quatre leçons au Collège de France* (Paris: Éditions Boutique de l'Histoire, 1999).

Monod, Gabriel. *Jules Michelet* (Paris: Sandoz et Fischbacher, 1875).

—. *Les Maîtres de l'histoire: Renan, Taine, Michelet* (Paris: Calmann Lévy, 1894).

—. *Jules Michelet. Études sur sa vie et ses oeuvres avec des fragments inédits* (Paris: Hachette, 1905).

—. *La Vie et la pensée de Jules Michelet (1798-1852)*, 2 vols. (Paris: Champion, 1923).

Moreau, Thérèse. *Le Sang de l'histoire. Michelet, l'histoire et l'idée de la femme au XIXᵉ siècle* (Paris: Flammarion, 1982).

Olivieri, Achille. *Il Laboratorio di Jules Michelet. Storia, tempo e immaginazione. Un saggio di metodologia* (Milan: Unicopli, 2001).

Orr, Linda. *Jules Michelet. Nature, History, and Language* (Ithaca, N.Y.: Cornell University Press, 1976).

Petitier, Paule. *Jules Michelet. L'homme histoire* (Paris: Grasset, 2006).

Quinet, Mme Edgar. *Cinquante ans d'amitié. Michelet-Quinet (1825-1875)* (Paris: Armand Colin, 1899).

Remaud, Olivier. *Michelet. La Magistrature de l'histoire* (Paris: Éditions Michalon, 1998).

Rudler, Gustave. *Michelet, historien de Jeanne d'Arc*, 2 vols. (Paris: P.U.F., 1925-1926).

Viallaneix, Paul. *La Voie royale. Essai sur l'idée du peuple dans l'oeuvre de Michelet* (Paris: Flammarion, 1971).

—, ed. *Michelet cent ans après. Études et témoignages* (Grenoble: Presses Universitaires de Grenoble, 1975). Essays by Viallaneix, Linda Orr, Jacques Seebacher, Jean-Pierre Richard, Pierre Malandain, Edward Kaplan, Louis Le Guillou, Simone Bernard-Griffiths, Elisabeth Brisson, Arimadavane Giovindane, François Papillard.

Williams, John R. *Jules Michelet. Historian as Critic of French Literature* (Birmingham, AL: Summa Publications, 1987).

Wilson, Edmund. "Michelet," *The New Republic* (31 August 1932).

—. *To the Finland Station: A Study in the Writing and Acting of History* (New York: Harcourt Brace, 1940).

Special numbers of the journals *L'Arc*, 52 (1973); *Europe*, 51, nos. 535-536 (1973); *Clio*, 6, no. 2 (1977); *Revue d'histoire littéraire de la France*, 74, no. 5 (1974).

This book does not end here...

At Open Book Publishers, we are changing the nature of the traditional academic book. The title you have just read will not be left on a library shelf, but will be accessed online by hundreds of readers each month across the globe. We make all our books free to read online so that students, researchers and members of the public who can't afford a printed edition can still have access to the same ideas as you.

Our digital publishing model also allows us to produce online supplementary material, including extra chapters, reviews, links and other digital resources. Find *On History* on our website to access its online extras. Please check this page regularly for ongoing updates, and join the conversation by leaving your own comments:

http://www.openbookpublishers.com/isbn/9781909254701

If you enjoyed the book you have just read, and feel that research like this should be available to all readers, regardless of their income, please think about donating to us. Our company is run entirely by academics, and our publishing decisions are based on intellectual merit and public value rather than on commercial viability. We do not operate for profit and all donations, as with all other revenue we generate, will be used to finance new Open Access publications.

For further information about what we do, how to donate to OBP, additional digital material related to our titles or to order our books, please visit our website, http://www.openbookpublishers.com.

OpenBook Publishers

Knowledge is for sharing

www.ingramcontent.com/pod-product-compliance
Lightning Source LLC
Chambersburg PA
CBHW070910030726
47504CB00005B/1537